VIRGINIA
Vignettes

VOLUME 1

Famous Characters & Events
in Central Virginia History

RICK BRITTON

ALSO BY RICK BRITTON

Jefferson: A Monticello Sampler

Albemarle & Charlottesville: An Illustrated History

VIRGINIA
Vignettes

VOLUME 1

Famous Characters & Events
in Central Virginia History

RICK BRITTON

Cedar Creek Publishing
Virginia, USA

VIRGINIA
Vignettes

VOLUME 1
Famous Characters & Events
in Central Virginia History

Copyright © 2015 by Rick Britton

Published by
Cedar Creek Publishing
Virginia, USA
www.cedarcreekauthors.com

Connect with us!
Facebook.com/CentralVirginiaHistoryBlast
Facebook.com/CedarCreekPublishing
Twitter @VirginiaBooks
Pinterest.com/ccpublishing

Printed in the United States of America

ISBN 978-1-942882-02-2

Library of Congress Catalog Number 2015933868

Contents

Introduction

Central Virginia history is permeated with fascinating stories and larger-than-life individuals. Three central Virginians have of course led our nation, but another—a great lady possessed of extraordinary wit and charm—established the country's standards of decorum and hospitality. Central Virginia has never lacked literary talent, but one particular resident penned dark and twisted tales that have delighted the world. Another stamped his imprint onto the rough-hewn American West. Central Virginians, too, struggled successfully against adversity, and lifted themselves up out of gut-wrenching poverty and the horror that was slavery. They also fought and died in our nation's conflicts; in the process confounding the British, and helping defeat the twentieth century's greatest evil—Nazi Germany. Truly amazing people, these central Virginians. They've left us a legacy few other regions can match.

Virginia Vignettes: Famous Characters & Events in Central Virginia History (Volume I) is akin to the wonderful annuals published by Virginia's many fine historical societies. Instead of focusing on just one county, however, *Virginia Vignettes* claims as its region all of central Virginia. As you've already gathered, this book is the first in a series: no one volume could possibly contain *all* of central Virginia's best stories.

These essays, in earlier incarnations, have all appeared elsewhere. They've all since been re-written, re-edited, and now, for the first time, endnoted. I take this opportunity to thank the stupendous editors I've had the pleasure to write for: Mary Sproles Martin, Jamie Miller, Hilary Weiss Swinton, Kathleen Valenzi Knaus, Bill Miller, Robert Viccelio, Frank Grizzard, and Hawes Spencer. For this little volume, a special thanks is due Montpelier's Hilary Hicks, who expertly fact-checked the Dolley Madison essay.

While I stand in awe of the central Virginians who have gone before us, I dedicate this volume of *Virginia Vignettes* to my beautiful wife Victoria, without whose love and support nothing would be possible.

Rick Britton
Charlottesville, Virginia

A narrow track through Virginia woods.
(Photo by Victoria Britton.)

From Cuckoo Tavern to Charlottesville:
Jack Jouett's Overnight Ride

Because the heat was oppressive, and perhaps because the dinner and drink sat heavy in his gut, John Jouett, Jr., curled up beneath the great elm in the yard at Cuckoo Tavern to catch a few winks. Despite the revelry droning on in the background, "Jack," as his friends called him, was soon fast asleep.[1] It was the moonlit evening of June 3, 1781—a Sunday. The American Revolution was in its seventh spring.

Startled awake at 10:00 p.m., Jouett peered into the moonlight toward the steadily approaching clatter. The sight was absolutely terrifying; a 250-man British raiding party—dragoons and mounted infantrymen—that filled the dusty roadway for 200 yards. At the head trotted green-jacketed horsemen whose very name had grown infamous. They were the British Legion, loyalists from New Jersey, Philadelphia, and New York City; hardened Americans who had sworn allegiance to King George. At the Waxhaws in May of 1780, these dragoons, sabers slashing, had hacked their way through Virginia Continentals attempting to surrender. Dozens were massacred.

Bobbing alongside the vanguard was the Legion's commander, Lieut. Col. Banastre Tarleton, a twenty-six-year-old Liverpudlian who had risen in the ranks thanks to fast riding, hard fighting, and a ruthlessly aggressive nature. To the Americans this "Green Dragoon" was a butcher—"Bloody Ban." And since the Waxhaws "Tarleton's Quarter!" had become a patriot rallying cry; it meant death to enemy

11

troops with their hands in the air. To the British, however, Banastre Tarleton was "a capital horseman, the very model of a partisan leader."[2]

Jouett instantly surmised Tarleton's destination. The road fronting Cuckoo Tavern ran northwesterly to Louisa Court House, then onward to the gap in the Southwest Mountains at Pantops (a distance of about forty miles). Just beyond sat the previously unimportant backwater town of Charlottesville. Now, however, Charlottesville was serving as the temporary state capital because three weeks earlier, at the approach of the enemy, the entire government—both houses of the legislature and Governor Thomas Jefferson—had fled Richmond for points west. This, Jack knew, because his father, John Jouett, Sr., was the proprietor of Charlottesville's Swan Tavern, just across from the courthouse. At that very moment, no doubt, a number of the unsuspecting assemblymen were sampling Jouett Senior's fare.

Understanding the dire circumstances—Virginia's civil leadership, in its entirety, was seemingly Tarleton's for the taking—Jack Jouett mounted his horse and set off for Charlottesville. He was one rider, alone, on a mission to thwart one of his country's most despised, and feared, enemy commanders. The Revolutionary War had finally come to Virginia's backcountry Piedmont.

Unlike the legendary "Midnight Ride" of Bostonian Paul Revere—much celebrated in poetry, paintings, and even U. S. postage stamps—Jack Jouett's overnight race from Cuckoo to Charlottesville remains relatively obscure. Perhaps it's because Jouett, unlike Revere, was not already famous or well-to-do when he performed his heroic feat. And perhaps it's because Jack Jouett, after the war, sought his fortune out on the newspaper-sparse frontier, away from the centers of population and publicity. Whatever the reason, however, the central Virginian's desperate dash, under the light of scrutiny, far outshines Revere's. Thanks to Jack Jouett's forty-mile ride, four signers of the Declaration of Independence escaped capture. So did a future president, the father of another future president, and the state's chief executive (among many others). What seems most remarkable about this episode is that the Old Dominion, supposedly the country's most powerful state, had buckled so quickly under the enemy's blows. And that the entire administration was skeddadling like a pack of frightened geese. For Revolutionary Virginia, this was the time that tried men's souls.

How had the situation gotten so grim? Amazingly, for the war's first six years, Virginia—by far the most populous state—remained relatively unscathed. That changed quickly during the first five months of 1781; coincidentally the last five months of Jefferson's second one-year gubernatorial term. On December 30, 1780, the traitor Benedict Arnold—now an enemy general—sailed up the James River with 1,800 men aboard twenty-seven British warships. The new capital at Richmond, with its military supplies and tobacco-packed warehouses, was the obvious target. "When the general panic set in," wrote historian John E. Selby, "the governor fled from the city with his family in the early morning hours of January 5, an action occasioning charges of cowardice that plagued him throughout his political career."[3] Arnold captured the city that afternoon. Two weeks later, after much burning and looting at Richmond and along the James, Arnold sailed downstream to Portsmouth and dug in.[4] Meanwhile, all across Virginia, county lieutenants attempted to muster their militiamen. Too few turned out.

Two months later a British fleet landed over 2,000 reinforcements at Portsmouth. Over the course of April, the British launched a number of raids, and actions were fought all along the James—including a battle at Blandford (near Petersburg), and a one-sided naval contest at Osborne's on the James River. There, on the twenty-seventh, the entire Virginia navy was lost, including—perhaps prophetically—the *Jefferson*, which was scuttled.[5] When the British again advanced against Richmond on April 30, the capital was rescued, at the eleventh hour, by Maj. Gen. Marquis de Lafayette at the head of 900 northern Continentals dispatched from George Washington's army (posted outside of New York City). For the next month this force—augmented by some 1,500 untested militiamen—was the largest the Old Dominion could muster. When Gen. Charles Lord Cornwallis marched into Virginia from North Carolina with 1,500 additional British soldiers, and another 1,500 arrived by sea, the twenty-four-year-old Lafayette was suddenly greatly outnumbered. Facing him was a consolidated British field army of about 7,200 veterans. And the new leader, Cornwallis, was an experienced and aggressive officer.[6] In the course of but a few months, Virginia had become the war's most active theater of operations.

"Cornwallis was not an aristocratic dilettante," explained historian Andrew O'Shaughnessy, "he was a real military professional. He was also a gambler, someone willing to take major risks. He essentially wanted to make Virginia collapse."[7] Surprisingly, the Old Dominion seemed willing to acquiesce. On May 10, because of the deteriorating military situation, the Virginia legislature determined to quit the state capital and reconvene in Charlottesville, beyond the Southwest Mountains.

Lafayette also abandoned Richmond when Cornwallis advanced a few weeks later. Frustrated at his inability to ensnare Lafayette, the forty-three-year-old Britisher decided instead to raid into Virginia's interior. Knowing that the governor and the legislature had fled to Charlottesville, and knowing that from that point they would call out more state troops, Cornwallis ordered Tarleton—the brilliant and brutal cavalryman—"To frustrate these intentions, and to distress the Americans, by breaking up the assembly. . . ."[8]

Early on June 3, Lieutenant Colonel Tarleton set out from Hanover Court House, north of Richmond, with 180 horsemen from his own Legion augmented by seventy mounted infantrymen from the 23rd Regiment, the Royal Welsh Fusiliers. These improvised horsemen, foot soldiers atop horseflesh stolen from the Virginia countryside, rode with their light muskets slung across their red tunics. Because the weather was exceedingly warm, the going was slow. Tarleton's column, in fact, took up most of the first day to reach Cuckoo Tavern, a distance of about thirty miles.

Jack Jouett's thoughts can only be imagined as he espied the enemy raiders. Disregarding his own safety, however, the Virginian was immediately concerned for his country, and his country's government. Fortunately his bay mare Sally—"the fleetest steed in seven counties"—was nearby in the tavern's paddock.[9] Quickly donning his riding boots, scarlet jacket, and plumed military cap, Jouett was soon cantering down the highway at a safe distance behind Tarleton's column.[10] Somehow he had to beat them to Monticello and Charlottesville. It was a dangerous proposition, no doubt, and Jouett had no way of knowing if anyone else was similarly engaged on that moonlit night. If he was indeed acting alone, the Old Dominion's fate was resting on the evening's visibility, and Jouett's knowledge of the wilderness trails. Providence could not have selected a better messenger.

Born in Albemarle County on December 7, 1754, the twenty-six-year-old Jack Jouett, Jr. has often been described as "intelligent, resourceful, daring, and brave."[11] He was also a strapping young fellow, according to Joel Meador, executive director of the Jack Jouett House in Versailles, Kentucky: "He stood six feet four inches tall, and weighed about 220 pounds. He was the son of a tavern owner."[12] Indeed, the running of wayside taverns—a lucrative business in the days when friendly stopping-places were few—seems to have been in the Jouett family blood. In 1742 Jack's grandfather, Matthew Jouett, had opened an "ordinary" in his house near present-day Louisa.[13] Matthew's son—John Jouett, Sr., Jack's father—had once been the owner of Cuckoo Tavern itself. After selling that establishment in 1773, Jouett Senior purchased "one hundred acres adjoining [Charlottesville] on the east and north, and at that time most likely erected the Swan Tavern, of famous memory."[14] During the

Revolution he acted as a commissary, selling "considerable beef and other needed supplies . . . to the quartermasters of the Continental Army."[15]

Patriotism, evidently, was also a dominant trait in this French Huguenot family, although the standard story—that Jack "was a captain in the Virginia militia, as were his three brothers," Matthew, Robert, and Charles—does not hold up under close examination.[16] A search of the state's militia records revealed no Capt. John Jouett.[17] Instead, one of the earliest accounts referred to Jack as a "showy gentleman" who "was no officer," but had "an eccentric custom" of wearing military-style getup.[18] Two brothers, however, *were* captains in the Virginia Continental Line—the regular army at the time— older brother Matthew in the 7th Virginia Regiment, and Robert in Col. James Wood's 12th Virginia. With two Jouetts serving in the Continental Army, Jack and his father evidently felt compelled to make a political statement. In June of 1779 both signed the curious Albemarle "Declaration of Independence" which stated in part that: "we renounce . . . all Allegiance to George the third . . . [and] will be faithfull & bear True Allegiance to . . . Virginia as a free & independent state. . . ."[19]

Freedom and independence were certainly at stake as Jouett, an excellent horseman, trotted in the wake of Tarleton's troopers. Moving cautiously once he neared Louisa Court House, Jouett "could see dimly the dragoons moving about."[20] The raiders had halted to water their horses. Polished buttons, and especially metal-sheathed sabers, reflected under the bright moonlight. Tarleton wrote that he "halted at eleven near Louisa Court House, and remained on a plentiful plantation till two o'clock."[21] The best road to Charlottesville blocked, Jouett "turned Sally into an abandoned road by way of which the logs for the Court House had been brought. He knew the trail well, having hunted along it."[22]

In the eighteenth century, central Virginia *was not* a region crisscrossed by numerous well-maintained roads. The best trails running east-to-west through the dense wilderness, in fact, were that being used by the British, and to its south, across the South Anna River, the Three Notched Road leading from Richmond to the Shenandoah. To best outstrip Tarleton, therefore, Jouett headed southwestward, toward the trail whose famous signposts—trees bearing three hatchet chops, like chevrons—would thereafter guide him to Charlottesville. This meant traversing logging trails and seldom-used cow paths. "His progress was greatly impeded by matted undergrowth, tangled brush, overhanging vines and gullies. . . . [H]is face was cruelly lashed by tree limbs as he rode forward and scars said to have remained the rest of his life were the result of lacerations sustained from these low hanging branches."[23]

Drenched with sweat, Jouett splashed into the South Anna somewhere south of Louisa Court House. Perhaps he stopped briefly to water Sally, and perhaps he even washed off her flanks, now covered with scratches. Soon he was back in the saddle. "He could judge by the position of the moon that the night was far spent, causing him to travel faster. . . . He was determined to beat Tarleton or die in the effort."[24] Within a few miles, horse and rider stumbled into Three Notched Road. Heading west along this well-marked byway, Jouett spurred Sally to even greater efforts. They still had twenty-five miles to go.

Tarleton's force was on the move again at 2:00 a.m. Before daylight, the marauders captured and burned twelve wagons carrying weapons and clothing for the Continental Army. Just after daybreak, wrote Tarleton, "some of the principal gentlemen of Virginia, who had fled . . . to the mountains for security, were taken out of their beds."[25] At Castle Hill, the estate of Dr. Thomas Walker—discoverer of the Cumberland Gap into Kentucky—the British cavalrymen rested for half an hour. (This brief stopover has been the subject of numerous tall tales. Most all involve an elaborate, delaying breakfast. In one version, for example, Walker's cook took up a significant amount of Tarleton's precious time preparing him a huge meal. In another, the first meal was snatched away by hungry horsemen, requiring the cook to prepare another. None of these fabrications should be believed. Tarleton was an experienced cavalry leader engaged in a raid that represented his greatest wartime opportunity. He would not have fallen for these obvious ruses.) Nearby a member of the Continental Congress, Frances Kinloch, was captured.[26]

Crossing the Rivanna at Milton, Jouett ascended Monticello Mountain three weary miles later. It was 4:30, "a little before sunrise."[27] Alerted, Jefferson's guests—members of the assembly plus the speakers of both houses—"breakfasted at leisure" then proceeded to Charlottesville.[28] Legend has it that Jefferson offered up a glass of fortifying Madeira when Jouett remounted to spread the alarm. Jefferson, however, was unhurried. Perhaps it was because his ill-fated governorship had ended two days earlier. (This meant, of course, that at the moment Virginia had no chief executive.) After sending off his family, and carefully organizing his papers, Jefferson was warned *again* of the British approach before he finally galloped up the adjoining wooded slope. He was mere minutes ahead of loyalist dragoons under Capt. Kenneth McLeod. Jefferson later referred to this extremely troubling episode—the so-called "Affair of Carter's Mountain"—as the very nadir of his political career.

Little Charlottesville, in the meantime, was a blur of activity. Warned by Jouett, the assemblymen quickly convened and decided to meet again three days later in Staunton, forty miles further west. Then they scattered. After dispatching McLeod to Monticello, Tarleton charged through a small militia force at Secretary's Ford on the Rivanna, then thundered onto courthouse square "to apprehend, if possible, the governor and assembly."[29] Most of the flock, of course, had flown. "Seven members of the assembly were secured," wrote Tarleton, neglecting to list their names, "and several officers and men were killed, wounded, or taken."[30] During their one-day stay, the British discovered "a great quantity of stores," and destroyed "one thousand firelocks . . . [u]pwards of four hundred barrels of powder" and "[s]everal hogsheads of tobacco. . . ."[31]

Jack Jouett's other activities that morning are difficult to sort out. Jefferson biographer Henry S. Randall wrote that Brig. Gen. Edward Stevens—wounded in battle and now serving in the legislature—was able to elude British dragoons because he was dressed as a Virginia farmer, and mounted on a shabby horse. "Mr. Jouett," however, thanks to his ersatz military attire, "was more attractive game" so the enemy took off after him instead. "After [Jouett] had coquetted with his pursuers long enough, he gave his fleet horse the spur, and speedily he was out of sight."[32]

Daniel Boone—representing the massive western county of Kentucky—was among the legislators in Charlottesville that day. Nathan Boone, Daniel's youngest son, related the following seventy years later: "[W]hen Jack Jouett gave notice of Tarleton's approach, my Father . . . remained, loading up on wagons the public records. . . . [W]hen they were overtaken by the British, questioned hastily, and dismissed. . . . [Jouett] called out, 'Wait a minute, Captain Boone, and I'll go with you.'" An enemy officer then said "Ah, is he a captain?" and took Boone into custody.[33] Conveyed to the British camp east of town, and held overnight in a coal house, the legendary frontiersman was reportedly interrogated by Tarleton and released. The two stories are difficult to square, they're contradictory. One has Jouett completely overlooked by the British—despite shooting off his mouth—while the other has him racing away from Charlottesville because his military garb made him more noticeable. Did either of these events take place? We'll probably never know.

What we do know is this: On June 15, 1781, just two weeks later, the assemblymen resolved that Jouett should receive "an elegant sword and pair of pistols as a memorial of the high sense which the General Assembly entertain of his activity and enterprise. . . ."[34] Jack Jouett got the pistols in 1783, but his receipt of the sword was delayed twenty years. By that time he'd made quite a name for himself out on the frontier. Jouett had managed Swan Tavern for a spell, then, like thousands of other Virginians, he lit out for Kentucky in 1782.

Two years later he married Sallie Robards, a relative of President Andrew Jackson's wife. The couple had twelve children. In 1787, and again in 1790, Jouett represented his region of Kentucky in the Virginia General Assembly. The year Kentucky gained statehood, 1792, Jouett was elected to represent Mercer County in the new state legislature. Three years later he represented Woodford County. Jouett was an agricultural leader as well; he imported livestock in large numbers and thus helped the Bluegrass State achieve its cattle- and horse-breeding fame.

In Kentucky, Jack Jouett is remembered as a high liver, a man full of humor and fun. Remarkable for his hospitality, Jouett was "the associate and companion of Henry Clay and Andrew Jackson . . . indeed of all the great men of early Kentucky."[35] He was a man of note in his day.

Jack Jouett died at Peeled Oak, his Bath County, Kentucky, farm, on February 21, 1822. He was buried in the nearby family cemetery, where unfortunately, "all the stones have been lost."[36] Somehow it seems fitting. Jack Jouett, the central Virginia patriot whose amazing Revolutionary War deed has been lost to history, now lies lost out on the Kentucky frontier. Even in death, he's still very much a mystery.

Endnotes

1. Tapp, Hambleton, "Jouett's Desperate Ride, The Lost Chapter of the American Revolution: Jack Jouett, Virginian, Kentuckian, *University of Kentucky Magazine* (Lexington, _____), pg. 6. Accounts differ as to Jouett's location when Tarleton rode past. Some say at the tavern; others place him at his father's farm in Louisa County nearby.

2. Sargent, Winthrop, quoted in Britton, Rick, *Jefferson; A Monticello Sampler* (Buena Vista, 2008), pg. 24.

3. Selby, John E., *The Revolution in Virginia, 1775-1783* (Williamsburg, 1988), pg. 223.

4. Ibid., pg. 224.

5. Ibid., pg. 273.

6. Ibid., pgs. 274-76.

7. Interview with Andrew O'Shaughnessy on 1/21/11. An authority on British commanders during the Revolution, O'Shaughnessy is the Saunders Director of the Robert H. Smith International Center for Jefferson Studies.

8. Tarleton, Banastre, *A History of the Campaigns of 1780 and 1781* (London, 1787), pg. 223.

9. Tapp, "Jouett's Desperate Ride," pg. 7.

10. Randall, Henry S., *The Life of Thomas Jefferson* (New York, 1858), pgs. 336-37. A very different portrait of Jack Jouett was painted by the earliest chroniclers of his feat. Randall, one of Jefferson's first serious biographers, claimed that much of his information had been gleaned from interviewing descendants of the Jefferson/Randolph family.

11. Tapp, "Jouett's Desperate Ride," pg. 7.

12. Joel Meador phone interview conducted on 1/07/11.

13. Unattributed, "The Jouett Story," in the files of the Jack Jouett House. In early Virginia, an "ordinary" was a "tavern" or an "inn," the names were interchangeable.

14. Woods, Edgar, *Albemarle County in Virginia* (Charlottesville, 1901), pgs. 241-42.

15. Dabney, Virginius, "Jack Jouett's Ride," *American Heritage Magazine* (December, 1961), Vol. 13, Issue 1.

16. Ibid.

17. McAllister, J. T., *Virginia Militia in the Revolutionary War* (Hot Springs, 1913). This is the standard reference work, and it lists every Virginia captain. "Jewett" was a variant spelling of "Jouett," but likewise there is no Capt. John (or Jack) Jewett listed.

18. Randall, *The Life of Thomas Jefferson*, pg. 337. Perhaps young Jack was jealous of his brothers? Several accounts refer to his odd habit of wearing military getup. He would not have been described this way if he were an actual captain. Most likely, he was described once as a "captain," and this was copied by other historians and writers. Also, in Kentucky Jack applied for the military pension owed his brother Matthew, not for his own.

19. See http://va.genealogy.tripod.com/declaration.txt for transcription and a complete list of signers.

20. Tapp, "Jouett's Desperate Ride," pg. 7.

21. Tarleton, *A History of the Campaigns*, pg. 296.

22. Tapp, "Jouett's Desperate Ride," pg. 7.

23. Dabney, Virginius, "Jouett Outrides Tarleton," *Scribner's Magazine* (June, 1928), Vol. 83, pgs. 690-98.

24. Tapp, "Jouett's Desperate Ride," pg. 8.

25. Tarleton, *A History of the Campaigns*, pg. 296.

26. Ibid.

27. Randall, *The Life of Thomas Jefferson*, pg. 336.

28. Ibid.

29. Tarleton, *A History of the Campaigns*, pg. 297.

30. Ibid.

31. Ibid.

32. Randall, *The Life of Thomas Jefferson*, pgs. 336-37.

33. Faragher, John Mack, ed., *My Father, Daniel Boone: the Draper Interviews with Nathan Boone* (New York, 1992), pg. 73.

34. Quoted in Dabney, "Jack Jouett's Ride."

35. Collins, Lewis, *Historical Sketches of Kentucky* (Mercer County, 1968), pgs. 619-20.

36. Joel Meador interview.

Dolley Payne Todd Madison (1768 – 1849).
(Courtesy of the Montpelier Foundation,
James Madison's Montpelier.)

Dolley Madison at Montpelier:
The Very Essence of Fine Virginia Hospitality

"That all-softening, overpowering knell,
The tocsin of the soul—the dinner bell."
  – From *Don Juan*
    by Lord Byron (1788-1824)

The previous day—March 4, 1817—had been fair and mild in Washington City, the federal capital. And quite momentous. Among the throng of 8,000 assembled for the inauguration of the fifth president of the United States, American citizens, recent immigrants, and foreign dignitaries alike vied for a better view of the tall Virginian. Because the Senate and the House of Representatives had disagreed as to the proper venue for the ceremony, James Monroe became the first chief executive sworn in out-of-doors.

That evening, after a formal reception, a lavish inauguration ball had been held in the home at the corner of "the Seven Buildings"— the temporary president's house at the intersection of Nineteenth Street and Pennsylvania Avenue. It had been a splendid night filled with hand-shaking, toast-drinking, and much high-flown political crowing. (The very fact that such a celebration was taking place, while nearby the official executive mansion was still under restoration following its torching in 1814, helped prove the resiliency of this brash, new democracy.)

But every such ringing-in, of course, must witness a concomitant ringing-out. James and Dolley Madison, the exiting presidential couple, remained in the capital long enough to bestow their blessings, and their fond farewells, on the myriad crowded gatherings. It was on occasions such as this that the much-loved Dolley "glided into the stream of conversation and accommodated herself to its endless variety," as noted famed Washington journalist Joseph Dennie. "[H]ow admirably the air of authority was softened by the smile of gayety."[1]

For the Madisons, the fifth of March was a day given over to packing. Dolley assisted her husband, seventeen years her senior, with the piles of personal papers and books. The leather-bound volumes were wrapped in paper and packed into wooden crates. His letters were organized chronologically and carefully consigned to specially marked trunks. All the while the forty-eight-year-old president's wife looked forward to their retirement at Montpelier with eager anticipation.

In one such moment of reflection, a house servant presented Dolley with a beautifully inscribed envelope. She immediately recognized the hand as that belonging to her longtime intimate friend, Eliza Collins Lee. She seated herself in a Windsor chair—the room's only uncluttered haven—broke the wax seal, and unfolded the missive.

"My Dear Friend," began the letter dated inauguration day, "On this day eight years ago, I wrote . . . to congratulate you on the joyful event that placed you in the highest station our country can bestow. . . . But the period has at length arrived when we must again part. You will retire . . . to your favorite retreat in Orange and will carry with you principles and manners not to be put off with the robe of state. . . . Talents such as yours were never intended to remain inactive. . . . You will cherish them, my dear friend, in a more native soil, [and] they will constitute the chief felicity of your dear venerated husband. . . ."[2]

During James Madison's presidency, 1809-1817, Dolley Madison created and defined the role of the First Lady. "[S]he is believed to have made a greater contribution to the social life of the country than any other woman who has had the honor of living in the White House."[3] As "the Nation's Hostess"—the undisputed heart of Washington society—she successfully employed her "principles and manners" toward the charming of the world. At Montpelier, in central Virginia, from her husband's retirement until his death, she continued in the role for which she was, according to her friend Mrs. Lee, "so peculiarly fitted." At the beautiful Piedmont estate Dolley Payne Madison's "talents"—her intelligence, her grace, her charisma—defined the very essence of Virginia plantation hospitality.

Relatives, friends, admirers, and political associates came to Montpelier by the score. "People loved to be here," explained Montpelier's former director of curatorial operations. "Madison really became known as the 'Sage of Montpelier'—people came to talk to him, to learn from Madison. And then they got comforted by Dolley." And oh, what an experience that was. "She was charming, outgoing, witty, very smart, but in a social way. She put everybody at ease. She never wore her intelligence on her shoulders, as it were, she was more concerned to see if you were happy, and comfortable."[4]

"During the entire period of Madison's retirement," wrote Dolley biographer Maud Wilder Goodwin, "the gates of Montpelier were never closed to friend or stranger. Visitors of every kind, impelled by every variety of motive, claimed entrance here, and had their claim allowed. . . . It was a principle at Montpelier that every guest be feasted—'if a stranger, because strangers ought to be made to pass their time as agreeably as possible; if a friend, because nothing can be too good for one's friends.'"[5] A domestic policy of this nature, of course, is sure to encourage even the most remote of acquaintances.

The beauty of the home and its environs, too, visitors found very enticing. The first version of the home—on a site well-chosen among the estate's 4,000 acres—was built by the president's father between 1763 and 1765. Following the death of his younger brother

Ambrose in 1793, the responsibility of managing Montpelier fell largely on James Madison.[6] Within the next seven years he transformed the Georgian structure into a much larger mansion in the neoclassical Federal style. A thirty-foot addition was attached to the house, and a west-facing front portico was built. Between 1809 and 1812, a rear colonnade was added to Montpelier, as well as one-story wings that included indoor basement kitchens. Just northwest of the house a handsome, classical garden temple was erected.[7]

For many of Montpelier's guests the long trip from Washington—three or four days by coach—served as a wonderful prelude for their encounter with the ex-president and his gracious wife. "The first stage of the journey is tedious and somewhat desolate, but as the road advances southward, the foothills of the mountains rise encouragingly before the eyes, the country begins to roll itself into green billows and in the distance, like stately sentinels, loom the cones of the Blue Ridge."[8] South of Orange, the road—after plunging through groves of thick-growing pines—at last "halts before an old-fashioned gateway, whose posts are topped with the always graceful urn. . . . The Montpelier homestead is a mansion. Before the eye has had time to take measures, it is assured of that fact."[9]

"It was near five o'clock when we arrived [at Montpelier]," wrote Margaret Bayard Smith of an 1809 visit. Mrs. Smith was a novelist married to the editor of Washington's *National Intelligencer*. "[W]e were met at the door by Mr. M[adison] who led us in to the dining room where some gentlemen were still smoking segars and drinking wine. Mrs. M. enter'd the moment afterwards, and after embracing me, took my hand, saying with a smile, I will take you out of this smoke to a pleasanter room. She took me thro' the tea room to her chamber which opens from it. Everything bespoke comfort, I was going to take a seat on the sopha, but she said I must lay down by her on her bed, and rest myself, she loosened my riding habit, took off my bonnet, and we threw ourselves on her bed. Wine, ice, punch and delightful pine-apples were immediately brought."[10]

Two of the first formal visitors during Madison's retirement were Sir Charles and Lady Bagot. Described as "a perfect gentleman," Bagot served as English Minister to the United States from the December of 1814 signing of the Treaty of Ghent, Belgium, until well into the Monroe presidency. Sir Charles Bagot was very impressed by the manner in which Dolley ran a household that was, according to Katharine Anthony, "half public and half private in its essential character." In his memoirs he granted her the highest possible European praise, writing that "She looked every inch a Queen."[11]

By comparison, ex-President Madison, whom Dolley seemingly towered over, was often described as small, awkward, and sickly-looking. "At least some of James Madison's diminutive appearance was due to his thin frame, while Dolley Madison was decidedly Rubenesque, with a large bosom and very erect carriage."[12] "She was a big woman, plump and very pretty. At the beginning of her husband's retirement, Dolley's beauty was fading but she didn't think so. In the 1820s through 1840s she wore gowns that other women had stopped wearing, but she wasn't ridiculed because she always looked so good. . . . She commanded respect."[13]

And she ruled supreme at Montpelier's many wonderful fetes. "They would take tables outside, and [if these were not enough] create more tables with planks and saw-horses. These would be covered with this incredible damask linen. Any kind of seat—Windsor chairs, fancy chairs, you name it—they would drag outside."[14]

"Yesterday we had ninety persons to dine with us at one table, fixed on the lawn under a thick arbor," Dolley penned of one event in 1816. "The dinner was profuse and handsome, and the company very orderly. . . . We had no ladies except Mother Madison, Mrs. Macon, and Nellie Willis. The day was cool and all quite pleasant. Half a dozen only staid all night, and are now about to depart."[15]

"Mother Madison," mentioned above, was Nellie Conway Madison, the ex-president's mother who resided at Montpelier—albeit in a separate wing, with her ancient carved and polished mahogany furniture—until her death in 1829 at the remarkable age of ninety-eight. In 1828 the aged Mrs. Madison told Margaret Bayard Smith that her knitting kept her busy and that her eyes—"thanks be to God"—had not failed her so she could still read. "But in other respects I am feeble and helpless, and owe everything to her," she said pointing to Dolley who was sitting nearby. "She is my mother now, and tenderly cares for all my wants."[16] Two other relatives were also frequently in residence at Montpelier; Dolley's sisters Anna Payne Cutts and Lucy Payne Washington Todd.

One of Dolley and James Madison's most famous visitors—aside from Thomas Jefferson, of course, who was a frequent guest—was the Marquis de Lafayette. In November of 1824, during his "Triumphal Tour" of the United States, the old revolutionary spent five days at Montpelier after visiting with Jefferson. "Like a Canterbury pilgrimage, the long cavalcade from Monticello in due time arrived. Lafayette; his son, George Washington; his secretary, Levasseur; various state and county dignitaries; the English [writer and reformer] Frances Wright and her sister . . . descended from their carriages." In a twinkling the numerous portmanteaus and trunks were off-loaded. "The cavalcade was immediately absorbed as it were, without leaving a trace."[17]

In front of Montpelier's blazing fireplaces, Madison and "the Hero of the Revolution" recalled their experiences during the War for Independence. But Lafayette, too, had more modern, of-the-moment issues to discuss. He was deeply troubled by the South's continuing reliance on slavery, its "Peculiar Institution." For her part, Frances Wright plied Mr. Madison with the ideas that would soon be published as her cumbersomely titled *Plan for the Gradual Abolition of Slavery in the United States without Danger of Loss to the Citizens of the South.*

Virtually on Lafayette's heels, Daniel Webster, along with Mr. and Mrs. George Ticknor, visited Montpelier for four days just before Christmas, 1824. Webster at the time was serving his second term as a congressman representing Massachusetts; Bostonian Ticknor was a Dartmouth-educated professor of law. "We breakfasted at nine," wrote Ticknor, "dined about four, drank tea at seven, and went to bed at ten; that is, we went to our rooms, where we were furnished with everything we wanted, and where Mrs. Madison sent us a nice supper every night and a nice luncheon every forenoon."[18] Payne Todd, Dolley's ne'er-do-well son from her first marriage, accompanied the visitors on long afternoon horseback rides across the beautiful estate. Ticknor characterized his treatment at Montpelier as "a hospitality which becomes one who has been at the head of a nation."[19] Webster, for his part, was impressed with Montpelier's air of success and plenty.

It's not surprising, perhaps, that these guests were so awed by the food served at Montpelier. As it was at any large Virginia estate, dining was something of a ceremony, and the dining room one of the mansion's most important chambers. "A dinner party at Montpelier was a distinct affair. The food on the table was always luxurious. . . . A state dinner produced three or four kinds of meat, three or four kinds of bread, fresh vegetables, fruit, pastry, champagne, and ice."[20] A casual guest—one who presented himself between meals—could expect to be immediately presented with punch, ice, wine, and succulent slices of pineapple.

Following the main meal the drawing room would often be clouded-over by the heavy smoke of the men's after-dinner "segars." The walls of this charming room, according to Margaret Bayard Smith, were "covered with pictures, some very fine, from the ancient masters, but most of them portraits of our most distinguished men, six or eight by [Gilbert Stuart]. The mantle-piece, tables in each corner and in fact wherever one could be fixed, were filled with busts, and groups of figures in plaster, so that this apartment had more the appearance of a museum of the arts than of a drawing-room."[21]

Visitors to Montpelier were often struck by Dolley and James Madison's differences—he was small and shy, she was full-figured and outgoing—but few failed to comment on the great partnership they had formed. "[H]is common sense and Dolley's magnetic charm were an unbeatable combination," wrote Robert Rutland, editor-in-chief of the Papers of James Madison.[22] Conover Hunt-Jones noted that "[h]eartache in love was one thing that Madison and Dolley . . . had in common."[23] In 1783, James Madison's fervent attentions had been spurned by his betrothed, Kitty Floyd, whose head was turned by a medical student's advances. In later years Madison, still pained by the experience, attempted to destroy all references to the affair. In her life Dolley, too, had suffered through seasons of sorrow.

Mrs. Madison was born to Quaker parents, John and Mary Coles Payne, on May 20, 1768, in Guilford County, North Carolina. The following year the family moved to Hanover County, Virginia. It was in central Virginia, therefore, that the future First Lady spent the majority of her childhood. At a Quaker school Dolley began her formal studies, for, unlike the prevailing custom of the time, "the egalitarian Society of Friends was enthusiastic about the education of women."[24] The Quaker course of study, which young ladies attended between the ages of eight and sixteen, included reading, mathematics, fancy sewing, French, geography, history, religion and, at times, the classics.

This well-rounded schooling proved extremely beneficial. Those who were later graced by her presence found her conversation quite stimulating. "She is a strong-minded woman, fully capable of entering into her husband's occupations and cares," penned English writer Harriet Martineau of Dolley during Madison's retirement, "and there is little doubt that he owed much to her intellectual companionship. . . ."[25]

In 1783, when Dolley was 15 years old, John Payne moved the family to Philadelphia. There the Paynes became prominent members of the large Quaker society. Six years later the southern charmer caught the eye of John Todd, a Quaker attorney. They were married in January of 1790, the year Philadelphia became the federal capital. Their first child, John Payne Todd, was born in February of 1792.

What began as a prosperous year, however, ended in disaster. Dolley's father died penniless after suffering several business failures. The following fall, however, was immeasurably worse. A yellow fever epidemic that swept through Philadelphia in October of 1793 claimed the lives of both of Dolley's in-laws and, on the 24th, that of her husband as well. Tragically, Dolley's second son, seven-week-old William Temple Todd, succumbed on the very same day.[26]

A similar litany of woe might have crushed another; but Dolley Payne Todd was a hardy individual. And her inheritance was substantial—all of her husband's property plus two-thirds of the items belonging to her in-laws. Soon there were suitors. "She was now [twenty-six]; still young in all her feelings. . . . [W]ithin a few months after her husband's death we see her the centre of her little social world . . . universally admired. . . ."[27] Dolley was so attractive that, the story goes, gentlemen in Philadelphia would station themselves where they could admire her strolling by.

On one of these walks, in May of 1794, she was espied by forty-three-year-old James Madison, the illustrious Virginia congressman already famous as the principal framer of the Constitution. Shortly thereafter an excited Dolley wrote to her confidant Eliza Collins: "Dear Friend, thou must come to me— Aaron Burr says that the great little Madison has asked to be brought to see me this evening."[28] They were married that September.

Thirty-one years later the Madisons were still very much in love—and they were still much like the presidential couple that had hosted the masses. In 1825, a visit to Montpelier by thirty-four-year-old American writer Lydia Sigourney—"the sweet singer of Hartford"—inspired a poem. "[A] more celebrated lady than Lydia Sigourney did not exist in the country.... [During her life] she poured out a stream of poetical and prose works which formed the delight of innumerable readers."[29] Lydia and Dolley had much in common. They were two of the best-known American women at the time and yet neither appeared spoiled by celebrity.

Mrs. Sigourney's tribute to the beautiful Virginia estate, as well as its political sage and charming matriarch, reads, in part:

> How fair beneath Virginia's sky,
>
> Montpelier strikes the traveler's eye,
>
> Emerging from its forest bower,
>
> Like feudal chieftain's ancient tower,
>
> With parks and lawns and gardens drest,
>
> In peaceful verdure proudly blest. . . .
>
> Here wisdom rests in sylvan shade,
>
> That erst an empire's councils swayed,
>
> And goodness, whose persuasive art
>
> So justly won that empire's heart.[30]

Ten years later, in 1835, James and Dolley Madison were visited by another female author, English-born Harriet Martineau. Writing about such diverse topics as Unitarianism, abolition, and mesmerism, Martineau—and her brother, a Unitarian preacher—had gained fame in England as leaders of liberal and progressive thought. In her *Retrospect of Western Travel* she devoted an entire chapter to the Madisons. By this time the eighty-four-year-old ex-president was suffering severely from rheumatism, and had shrunken, in body but not in mental capacity, to almost childlike proportions.

"He was in his chair, with a pillow behind him, when I first saw him," wrote Martineau, "his little person wrapped in a black silk gown; a warm gray and white cap upon his head, which his lady took care should always sit becomingly. . . . His voice was clear and strong, and his manner of speaking particularly lively, often playful. . . . Mrs. M. is celebrated throughout the country for the grace and dignity with which she discharged the arduous duties which devolve upon the President's lady."[31]

"[Dolley] looks just as she did twenty years ago," wrote U.S. Congressman Charles Ingersoll the following year, "and dresses in the same manner, with her turban and cravat; rises early and is very active, but seldom leaves the house, as her devotion to Mr. Madison is incessant, and he needs all of her constant attention."[32]

James Madison died at Montpelier on June 28, 1836. He was interred on the estate, at a small brick-walled cemetery within a mile of the house. "When I was [Dolley's] guest [at Montpelier] she was in excellent health and lively spirits," Martineau penned after Madison's death, "and I trust that though she has since lost the great object of her life, she may yet find interests enough to occupy and cheer many years of an honored old age."[33]

In the fall of 1837 Dolley moved to Washington City, leaving Montpelier in the hands of Payne Todd (a disastrous decision). In a home on Lafayette Square the sixty-nine-year-old widow of "the great little Madison," the adored first "First Lady," was once again at the center of the capital's active social scene. (Unfortunately, Payne Todd was unable to successfully manage Montpelier. Dolley sold the estate in August of 1844.)

Dolley Payne Madison died on July 12, 1849, at the age of eighty-one. "Beloved by all who personally knew her, and universally respected," read her obituary in Washington's *Daily Intelligencer,* "this venerable Lady closed her long and well-spent life with the calm resignation which goodness of heart combined with piety only can impart. . . . [W]herever she appeared, every one became conscious of the presence of the spirit of benignity and gentleness, united to all the attributes of feminine loveliness."[34] First placed in a Washington vault, her remains were eventually brought back to central Virginia and placed alongside those of her husband at Montpelier.

There—standing at the mansion's entrance, alongside the tall columns of the front portico—today's visitor can easily imagine the greatness that was once Montpelier, and the amazing woman whose hospitality, grace, and wit set the standard for a nation.

Endnotes

1. Dennie, Joseph, writing as "Oliver Oldschool" in *Port Folio*, a journal espousing classical republican values, as quoted in Goodwin, Maud Wilder, *Women of Colonial and Revolutionary Times; Dolly Madison* (New York, 1911), pgs. 199-200.

2. Eliza Collins Lee to Dolley Madison, March 4, 1817, see Clark, Allen Culling, ed., *Life & Letters of Dolly Madison* (Washington, D.C., 1914), pg. 203.

3. Dean, Elizabeth Lippincott, *Dolly Madison; The Nation's Hostess* (Boston, 1928), pg. 6.

4. Interview of Lee Langston-Harrison conducted September 24, 1999. Langston-Harrison is currently the director of the Museum of Culpeper History. She was at Montpelier from 1998 to 2006.

5. Goodwin, Maud Wilder, *Women of Colonial and Revolutionary Times; Dolly Madison* (New York, 1911), pg. 221.

6. Peterson, Merrill D., ed., *James Madison; A Biography in His Own Words* (New York, 1974), Vol. 2, pg. 214.

7. Hunt-Jones, Conover, *Dolley and the "Great Little Madison"* (Washington, D.C., 1977), pgs. 61.4.

8. Goodwin, *Dolly Madison*, pgs. 201-02.

9. Ibid., pg. 202.

10. Hunt, Gaillard, ed., and Smith, Margaret Bayard, *The First Forty Years of Washington Society: Portrayed By the Family Letters of Mrs. Samuel Harrison Smith* (New York, 1906), pg. 81.

11. Anthony, Katharine, *Dolly Madison; Her Life and Times* (Garden City, N.Y., 1949), pgs. 289-90.

12. Hunt-Jones, *Dolley and the "Great Little Madison,"* pg. 12.

13. Langston-Harrison interview.

14. Ibid.

15. Quoted in Goodwin, *Dolly Madison*, pg. 222.

16. Ibid., pg. 208.

17. Anthony, *Dolly Madison*, pg. 287.

18. Quoted in Peterson, Merrill D., ed., *The Founding Fathers, James Madison; A Biography in His Own Words* (New York, 1974), Vol. 2, pg. 367.

19. Ibid., pg. 368.

20. Anthony, *Dolly Madison*, pg. 288.

21. Smith, Margaret Bayard, *The First Forty Years of Washington Society* (New York, 1906), pg. 233.

22. Hunt-Jones, *Dolley and the "Great Little Madison,"* pg. xvii.

23. Ibid., pg. 10.

24. Ibid., pg. 7.

25. Anthony, *Dolly Madison*, pg. 298.

26. Hunt-Jones, *Dolley and the "Great Little Madison,"* pg. 9.

27. Goodwin, *Dolly Madison*, pg. 47.

28. Quoted in Goodwin, *Dolly Madison*, pg. 50.

29. Anthony, *Dolly Madison*, pg. 290.

30. Ibid., pg. 291.

31. Quoted in Anthony, *Dolly Madison*, pg. 295.

32. Quoted in Clark, Allen C., *Life and Letters of Dolly Madison* (Washington, D.C., 1914), pg. 271.

33. Quoted in Goodwin, *Dolly Madison*, pg. 234.

34. Quoted in Dean, *Dolly Madison*, pg. 241.

Edgar Allan Poe (1809 – 1849).

"A Multitude of Novel Follies":
Edgar Allan Poe at the University of Virginia

"The supposition that the book of an author is a thing
apart from the author's self is, I think, ill-founded. . . .
Of such a person we get, from his books, not merely a
just, but the most just representation."
— Edgar Allan Poe, 1846[1]

The clutch of well-groomed University students—seated around a large oval drop-leaf table in Monticello's dining-room—immediately quieted down as the resurfaced door from the parlor opened, slowly. Wide-eyed they stood, and turned, to greet the master of the household. One of them, a slender youth with the affected air of a Frenchman, fumbled with his cravat. Several others quickly brushed off their frocks. From atop the mantelpiece, as if in celebration of the occasion, the alabaster pillar clock began striking four. It was a spring afternoon in the year 1826—a Sunday.

As the eighty-three-year-old Thomas Jefferson entered the room the students stiffened, staring. He looked thin, frail, and disheveled. And, to the aspiring young scholars, his many-layered clothing seemed to have come from a far-distant time—an impression that merely added to his image as the very embodiment of the revolutionary spirit. He coughed. And his slippers loudly rasped the floor as he shuffled forward, piercing the moment's uncomfortable silence.

With the great man's approach, youthful anticipation seemed to fill the elegant dining room. But if the students were expecting

41

the ex-president to dine at their table, they were sorely disappointed. Instead, Jefferson continued past—glancing and nodding at them in recognition—and was escorted into his adjoining tea room. There he sat by himself, safely ensconced beneath the approving terra-cotta glances of his "most honourable suite": John Paul Jones, Benjamin Franklin, George Washington, and the Marquis de Lafayette.[2]

"Oh . . . he's not going to speak with us," whispered a student to the slender youth, the very French-looking Latin scholar. "How could we possibly compete with the likes of them," he continued, raising an eyebrow toward the busts.

"Of course he will," answered the seventeen-year-old Edgar Allan Poe, adjusting his waistcoat as he sat down. "There has been quite a lot of talk about these dinners. . . . The founder merely wishes to eat his vegetables in peace. Once this cloth is removed we shall retire to the parlor with our esteemed host . . . and our Madeira. Then we will have an interesting conversation."

Poe's companion seemed unconvinced. Nonetheless, the budding poet took a long sip of cider, and mentally composed his introduction to the "Sage of Monticello."

"Mr. Jefferson," he thought, imagining himself standing before the venerable patriot, "I am Edgar Allan Poe. I have had the opportunity, sir—through my father, John Allan, of Richmond—to make the acquaintance of one of your oldest and dearest friends, Gen. John Hartwell Cocke. . . ."

How would Jefferson have responded? What could they have discussed? Imagine the multitude of possibilities. The two greatest, the two best-known, individuals ever associated with the University of Virginia engaged in a tete-a-tete.[3]

Is the scene apocryphal? Absolutely . . . but it could have taken place. Charlottesville's own Virginius Dabney wrote that Poe "is presumed to have sat at Jefferson's table."[4] No less a historian than Dumas Malone, Jefferson's greatest biographer, described how the third president—during the University's first two sessions—"usually had some of [the students] for dinner on Sunday."[5] Although he did not sit with them at the main table because of his deafness, Jefferson, after the meal, would "converse with them as individuals . . . and probably treated them as peers."[6]

This habit of Jefferson's appears to have been common knowledge at the University. "[E]very Sunday," remembered George Tucker, U.Va.'s first professor of moral philosophy, "some four or five of the students dined with him. At these times [Jefferson] generally ate by himself in a small recess connected with the dining room; but, saving at meals, sat and conversed with the company as usual."[7]

One would hardly expect a "usual," or ordinary, discourse between the eighty-three-year-old Jefferson and the seventeen-year-old Edgar Allan Poe, both of whom had strong personalities. But what the above tableau best illustrates, perhaps, is how easy it is to spin stories surrounding the wonderfully fascinating Poe, future father of a number of literary genres. Certainly many others, over the years, were concocted concerning his ten months in the central Piedmont, at the University of Virginia. Thanks to the writings of his first biographer, for example, it was long accepted as fact that Poe, at U.Va., was a wild, dissolute youngster who did poorly in his classes, drank to excess, and gambled in the evenings with the other ne'er-do-wells. Because of his bad behavior, it was said that he was expelled. Bits of this fabrication have long-since been dispelled; but other pieces, amazingly, have resisted the light of proof and clung to the writer's reputation like hell-bred shadows refusing to dissipate. Poe himself, in two of his short stories, perhaps revealed some of his own innermost feelings about his time as a student at Jefferson's "academical village."

Born in Boston, Massachusetts, on January 19, 1809, Edgar Poe was the son of David Poe, Jr. and Elizabeth Arnold, an attractive and talented English actress. Father David disappeared sometime in 1810: Elizabeth passed away in Richmond, Virginia, on December 8, 1811.[8] Soon thereafter Poe—not quite three—was taken into the home of John Allan, a wealthy merchant and tobacco exporter, and partner in the Richmond-based firm of Ellis and Allan.

From the beginning Allan promised, and seemed determined, to give his foster-son a good education. Seven-year-old "Edgar Allan"—as he was then called—began his studies at a London boarding school in 1816. The following year he was sent to the Manor House School at Stoke Newington, England, overseen by the Reverend John Bransby. Many years later, Bransby told another student of his that Poe, as a youngster, had been "intelligent, wayward, and willful." Bransby added that the future poet "was a quick and clever boy and would have been a very good boy if he had not been spoilt by his parents. [They] allowed him an extravagant amount of pocket-money, which enabled him to get into all manner of mischief. . . ."[9]

Poe continued his education in Richmond, studying Latin and Greek at Joseph H. Clarke's from 1820 to 1823. He was then tutored for ten months, in that city, by a Mr. William Burke. Also, young Edgar, as preparation for entering the University of Virginia, kept his nose in his books through many months of special coaching.

Edgar Allan Poe signed-in at the University of Virginia on Tuesday, February 14, 1826, one of five students to do so that day—number 36 out of a final enrollment of 177. He was thirteen days late for the beginning of the University's second session. The institution's matriculation book, which still survives, clearly shows Poe's name—unfortunately not in his own hand—misspells his foster-father's name as "Allen," records his residence as Richmond, and discloses that he elected to attend two schools: Ancient and Modern Languages. Interestingly, the column to the far right, under "Remarks," is blank "and is *prima facie* evidence," according to Charles W. Kent, "that Poe did not at any time during the session sever his connection with the University [emphasis in the original]."[10] He was not expelled.

So, what exactly was Poe's record at the University of Virginia? We know from Jefferson's meticulously written schedule that Professor George Long's class in Ancient Languages ran from 7:30 to 9:30 a.m. on Mondays, Wednesdays, and Fridays. The list of topics addressed by Long included Hebrew, rhetoric, belles-lettres, ancient history, geography, and of course Greek and Latin. George Blaettermann's class—Modern Languages: French, German, Italian, Anglo-Saxon, and Spanish—met at the same time period on the days in between, and additionally Saturday.[11]

Professor Long, after final examinations were over in mid-December, reported to the faculty the names of the students who had excelled in Latin and French. On the list Edgar Allan Poe appears fourth out of the nineteen best students of "Senior Latin." Similarly, Blaettermann placed the writer sixth out of his eight young scholars most proficient in "Senior French." (Although it should be noted that this list was alphabetical.) According to William Wertenbaker— a fellow-student at the time who went on to become University librarian—Poe had excelled in the examinations, and this was a high honor. Wertenbaker added that under the existing University regulations, the future father of horror "would have graduated in [Latin and French], and have been entitled to diplomas."[12]

Although the list of subjects covered in each of his two classes may appear daunting, the willful young poet certainly was not overtaxed by the daily demands of his studies. Especially since he had taken on only two classes—rather than the customary three—due to an insufficiency of funds. And the fact that Poe, because of his earlier training, wrote Kent, "possessed a quick eye and an alert mind that made the perilous process of 'reading ahead' less hazardous for him."[13] How did he spend all of his extra time?

Much of it was passed in the library. The University's first collection of books was located in the front upstairs room of Pavilion VII, West Lawn. (Although sometime in October of 1826 the books were moved into the Rotunda's Dome Room.) Somehow this image comes easily—young Edgar Poe bent over a stack of literary classics tucked away in a fairly dark recess. Thomas Goode Tucker, who had been an intimate friend of Poe's, remembered their reading together in the library their favorite historians, as well as the works of Geoffrey Chaucer and Sir Walter Scott. Tucker, too, claimed that they would often copy for each other their favorite passages of poetry.[14]

A talented artist, Edgar Allan Poe spent some of his time sketching. The walls of his dormitory room on the University's West Range—ironically, No. 13 "Rowdy Row"—were often seen covered in charcoal and crayon sketches. This fact was verified by ex-student John Willis, as well as by Jesse Maury, who worked hauling cut wood for the University's young scholars. Thomas Bolling remembered seeing Poe copying onto his ceiling's plaster an interesting plate from a book of Byron's poems. Possessed of a fine hand for penmanship, Poe was also known to entertain his school chums by writing on small scraps of paper a seemingly impossible number of words.[15]

Also considered quite an athlete, the seventeen-year-old devoted some of his spare moments to exercise and competitive sports. Despite his slender frame the future father of the detective genre was described as being very active, and an expert in the gymnastic arts. In June of the previous year Poe swam against the powerful current of the James River from Ludlam's Wharf to Warwick, an impressive distance of six miles. He was a decent boxer and a swift runner. And Charles W. Kent noted that it was "probably here at the University" that Poe broad-jumped "twenty-one feet six inches on a level, with a running start of twenty yards." It is also possible that Edgar Allan Poe participated in an unofficial military drill class that was taught during that session by William Matthews, a former West Point cadet.[16]

His athleticism was also exhibited in his love for taking long, solitary hikes out into the Albemarle County countryside. Over the years, Poe aficionados have wondered whether any of the youngster's University experiences ever found their way into his work. His "A Tale of the Ragged Mountains"—published in *Godey's Lady's Book* in April of 1844—provides us with a resounding yes. Set in Charlottesville, Virginia, in 1827, the story's protagonist is Mr. Augustus Bedloe, a very peculiar and sickly individual being treated by a Dr. Templeton, "a convert, in great measure, to the doctrine of [Franz] Mesmer."[17] Suffering from neuralgia, Bedloe is "in the highest degree sensitive, excitable, enthusiastic" and is in the habit of taking "a very large dose" of morphine immediately after "a cup of strong coffee" each morning. Based, of course, on Poe's memory of the central Virginia landscape, he sends Bedloe "attended only by a dog, upon a long ramble among the chain of wild and dreary hills that lie westward and southward of Charlottesville, and are there dignified by the title of the Ragged Mountains."[18]

"I bent my steps immediately to the mountains, and, about ten, entered a gorge which was entirely new to me," wrote Poe from Bedloe's point of view. "I followed the windings of this pass with much interest. The scenery which presented itself on all sides, although scarcely entitled to be called grand, had about it an indescribable and to me a delicious aspect of dreary desolation. The solitude seemed absolutely virgin. . . . I was indeed the first adventurer—the very first and sole adventurer who had ever penetrated its recesses."[19]

Like the author's stay at the University of Virginia, "A Tale of the Ragged Mountains" was doomed to an unhappy ending. Edgar Poe pushed the inquisitive Mr. Bedloe deeper and deeper into the mountain chasm until he was teleported—in place and time—to the Indian city of Benares and the year 1780. There Bedloe is engulfed in "the insurrection of Cheyte Sing"—an uprising against British rule—and, in a dream-like state, is transmogrified into a desperately overwhelmed British officer named "Oldeb" who is subsequently punctured by arrows while attempting to drive back the swarming mob. Completely unnerved by this experience, poor Mr. Bedloe returns to Charlottesville where, undergoing treatment, he's accidently killed by a poisonous leech. (For this odious creature Poe uses the name "sangsue," a French derivation of the Latin *sanguisuga* meaning literally "bloodsucker.") "The poisonous sangsue of Charlottesville," notes Bedloe's obituary, "may always be distinguished from the medicinal leech by its blackness, and especially by its writhing or vermicular motions, which very nearly resemble those of a snake."[20] In the end it's revealed that, of course, "Oldeb" is "Bedloe" reversed, minus the "e."

Much literary speculation has been written regarding "A Tale of the Ragged Mountains," especially about Poe's incorporation of the mysterious Orient and the occult-like practice of Mesmerism, but its deeper meaning might be quite simple. The story could simply be analogous to the experience of a young man—like Poe, like Bedloe— shoved further and further into an existence, a life, that in the end proved unlivable. Certainly, after his ten months' stay at the University of Virginia, Edgar Allan Poe must have felt his possibilities beginning to narrow.

It would be interesting to speculate on who Poe was referring to when he wrote of the black, writhing bloodsucker of Charlottesville. Interesting, too, is Poe's description of the story's main character; a description that word-for-word sounds strikingly like himself as a young man. "His eyes were abnormally large," he wrote of Bedloe, "and round like those of a cat. . . . In moments of excitement the orbs grew bright to a degree almost inconceivable; seeming to emit rays, not of a reflected but of an intrinsic lustre, as does a candle or the sun. . . ."[21]

As in the passage above, there were many "moments of excitement" at the University of Virginia during the 1826 session. Soon after Poe's arrival, for example, there was a student riot that led the University to seek help from the local authorities. Fifty students, according to Poe, "travelled off into the woods & mountains—taking their beds & provisions along with them" in order to escape arrest.[22] The exaggeration of Poe's involvement in several such incidents led to, what became for a while, the commonly accepted description of his life at the University of Virginia. Indeed, the Reverend Rufus Wilmot Griswold—amazingly, Poe's literary executor, and one of his first biographers—described the young writer, the youngster attending U.Va., as a self-conceited person with "no moral susceptibility." (A Poe contemporary, Griswold worked as a journalist, editor, poet, and critic. A rivalry between the two began over Poe's rather severe criticism of a much-touted poetry anthology compiled by Griswold, then grew more heated when Griswold succeeded Poe as editor of *Graham's Magazine*. The two even fought over the attentions of a then-famous female poet: Frances Sargent Osgood.)

Griswold wrote Poe's obituary for the *New York Daily Tribune* in 1849 and expanded on its themes for a longer "Memoir of the Author" that accompanied his three-volume edition of *The Works of Edgar Allan Poe* published in 1850. At the University of Virginia, Poe, according to Griswold, "led a very dissipated life," and "was known as the wildest and most reckless student of his class. . . . [His] gambling, intemperance, and other vices, induced his expulsion. . . ."[23]

Fortunately, later biographers exposed Griswold for what he truly was—a bumbling, vindictive man unable to contain his animosity toward, and his jealousy of, Edgar Allan Poe (and his fabulous body of work). Griswold even went so far as to invent "facts" and forge letters and documents in order to create, as wrote Charles W. Kent, a "scurrilous and irresponsible indictment" of his former competitor.[24]

But what of Griswold's claims? As William Wertenbaker, who as a classmate probably saw Poe on a fairly regular basis, remembered: "[Poe] certainly was not habitually intemperate, but he may occasionally have entered into a frolic. I often saw him in the Lecture Room and in the Library, but never in the slightest degree under the influence of intoxicating liquors."[25] Thomas Goode Tucker, however, recalled that the mercurial Poe was "exceedingly fond of peach and honey," an alcoholic beverage quite popular with the young students (as were mint-slings, mixed and unmixed wine, toddies, eggnog, and Madeira). "It was not the taste of the beverage that influenced him;" continued Tucker, who presumably was writing from personal observation, "without a sip or smack of the mouth [Poe] would seize a full glass, without water or sugar, and send it home at a single gulp. This frequently used him up; but, if not, he rarely returned to the charge."[26] It seems likely that Poe—of a nervous and sensitive nature—drank occasionally and needed but little to appear much more inebriated than he actually was.

The University's second session—1826, the year Poe attended—was a rough one for the institution. The professors were certainly top-drawer but even the "Sage of Monticello" was well aware that many of the students were not. According to the ex-president, one third of the young men were hard-working and one third were fairly diligent. Another part, however, Jefferson wrote, were "idle ramblers incapable of application."[27] Boisterous parties and general rowdyism threatened to overcome the Lawn that year. Many young "scholars" were brought before the faculty and several were expelled.

But in all the records, wrote Kent, "we nowhere find any mention of the name of Edgar Poe: and when a long list of students summoned to appear before the Albemarle grand jury was made out Poe was not included, though many of his boon companions were. Poe was not, then, among the offenders known to University or civil law, but from the private testimony of his college mates it is evident that he did sometimes play seven-up and loo, his favourite games for money."[28]

Therein lies the rub. Edgar Allan Poe spent far too many evenings betting on his card-play, which, if we believe the evidence, must have been inept. William Wertenbaker wrote of an evening spent with the young poet, possibly Edgar Poe's last night at No. 13: "On this occasion [Poe] spoke with regret of the large amount of money he had wasted and of the debts he had contracted during the session. If memory is not at fault, he estimated his indebtedness at $2,000. . . ."[29] In a letter to John Allan written a few years later Poe scolded his foster-father for insufficiently funding his ten months at the University of Virginia. He had tried to borrow more, Poe claimed, but failing that "I became desperate, and gambled—until I finally involved myself irretrievably."[30]

When Allan retrieved his young charge at the termination of the year the wealthy merchant refused to make good the exorbitant debts, especially those racked up over the gaming table. Instead, he took Poe back to Richmond and placed him, temporarily, as a clerk in his business. The relationship between the two would never be the same.

Perhaps the toughest indictment of Poe's gambling at the University of Virginia came from the writer himself. In "William Wilson," first published in 1839 in *Burton's Gentleman's Magazine*, we find an Oxford student struggling against his wicked nature; a nature consumed with the very vice that brought about the end of Poe's studies at U.Va.—gambling. "William Wilson" commences with a retelling of Poe's own schooldays at Stoke Newington. Poe, for example, describes Stoke Newington's Manor House School in great detail—"a large, rambling, Elizabethan house, in a misty-looking village of England"—and even indentifies the headmaster as Bransby.[31] At the Manor House School the narrator encounters his double; a doppelganger really, with the same name, same birth date, and a very similar countenance. The ensuing conflict between the two William Wilsons continues until the narrator—the wicked of the two— dispatches his better half in a knife fight.

Literary critics have long considered the tale an allegory depicting an evil man's inner struggles with his better nature. But it's also possible that through "William Wilson" Edgar Allan Poe was revealing the pain he suffered at the realization of the opportunities he'd thrown away—and exactly how he'd lost them—at Mr. Jefferson's University. "Let it suffice . . ." explains the story's narrator, "that, giving name to a multitude of novel follies, I added no brief appendix to the long catalogue of vices then usual in the most dissolute university of Europe. . . . I had . . . so utterly fallen from the gentlemanly estate, as to seek acquaintance with the vilest arts of the gambler by profession, and, having become an adept in his despicable science, to practice it habitually . . . at the expense of the weak-minded among my fellow-collegians."[32] Here we see, perhaps, Edgar Allan Poe damning the vulture-like—or bloodsucking—nature of those who had preyed on his innocence in the after-hours at U.Va.

Edgar Allan Poe, in his brief career, created works of fiction which, to this day—many maintain—shine with a brilliance unmatched in that great, competitive galaxy of American literature. Because of his fame there is still much interest in his amazing life and, in particular—thanks to the vile pen of Rufus Wilmot Griswold—his time at the University of Virginia. "The name of Poe still has a kind of magic," wrote Floyd Stovall, "and the false image created by Griswold still survives in the popular mind. . . ."[33] Hopefully modern readers will search past the shadows, brush away the cobwebs, and discover for themselves the seventeen-year-old boy who once walked the U.Va. Lawn, hiked into the Ragged Mountains, and perhaps, just perhaps, discussed a mutual acquaintance with the "Sage of Monticello."

Endnotes

1. Poe, Edgar A., "The Literati of New York City.—No. IV.; Some Honest Opinions at Random Respecting Their Autorial Merits, With Occasional Words of Personality," *Godey's Lady's Book* (New York, August 1846), 33: 72.

2. This was the nickname Jefferson gave to his collection of busts mounted high in his tea room.

3. This imagined scene is based on accounts by Dumas Malone, Virginius Dabney, and George Tucker (see below), as well as my many years' experience as a guide on Jefferson's "little mountain."

4. Dabney, Virginius, *Mr. Jefferson's University* (Charlottesville, 1988), pg. 8.

5. Malone, Dumas, *Jefferson and His Time; The Sage of Monticello* (Boston, 1981), pg. 463.

6. Ibid.

7. Tucker, George, *Life of Thomas Jefferson* (Philadelphia, 1837), Vol. II, pg. 477.

8. Interestingly, Poe's mother is buried in the church-yard cemetery at St. John's in Richmond, the selfsame house of worship where Patrick Henry delivered his most famous speech.

9. Quinn, Arthur Hobson, *Edgar Allan Poe: A Critical Biography* (New York, 1941), pgs. 71-72. The Bransby student quoted by Quinn was William Elijah Hunter.

10. Kent, Charles W., "Poe's Student Days at the University of Virginia," *The Bookman Illustrated Magazine of Literature and Life* (New York, July 1901), Vol. 13, no. 5, pg. 431. "Chucky" Kent, as he was called, starting in 1893, held a chair in the University's "School of English Language and Literature." He remained for over a decade.

11. Stovall, Floyd, "Edgar Poe and the University of Virginia," *The Virginia Quarterly Review* (Charlottesville, Spring 1967), Vol. 43, No. 2, pgs. 297-99.

12. Wertenbaker, William, as quoted in Harrison, James Albert, "New Glimpses of Poe (II)," *The Independent* (New York, Sept. 13, 1900), Vol. LII, No. 2702, pgs. 2201-02.

13. Kent, "Poe's Student Days," pg. 434.

14. Ibid., pgs. 434-35.

15. Ibid., pg. 432.

16. Ibid., pgs. 431-32.

17. Poe, Edgar Allan, "A Tale of the Ragged Mountains," *Complete Tales & Poems of Edgar Allan Poe* (New York, 1938), pg. 680. In this edition this story only occupies pages 679 to 687.

18. Ibid.

19. Ibid., pg. 681.

20. Ibid., pg. 686.

21. Ibid., pg. 679.

22. Edgar Allan Poe to John Allan, May 1826. Cauthen, Irby B. Jr., *Edgar Allan Poe at the University* (Charlottesville, 1999), pg. 13. This was one of only two surviving letters penned by Poe to his foster-father while at U.Va. Unfortunately, he didn't record what day in May it was written.

23. Griswold, Rufus Wilmot, "Memoir of the Author," *The Works of the Late Edgar Allan Poe* (New York, 1850-56), Vol. 3, pg. ix.

24. Kent, "Poe's Student Days," pg. 438.

25. Wertenbaker, "New Glimpses of Poe (II)," pg. 2201.

26. Tucker, Thomas Goode, as quoted in Kent, "Poe's Student Days," pg. 543.

27. Thomas Jefferson to Robert Greenhow, July 24, 1825.

28. Kent, "Poe's Student Days," pg. 437.

29. Ibid., pgs. 439-40.

30. E. A. Poe to John Allan, January 3, 1831.

31. Poe, Edgar Allan, "William Wilson," *Complete Tales & Poems of Edgar Allan Poe* (New York, 1938), pg. 627. "William Wilson," in this edition, runs from page 626 to page 641.

32. Ibid., pg. 637.

33. Stovall, Floyd, "Edgar Poe and the University of Virginia," *The Virginia Quarterly Review* (Charlottesville, Spring 1967), Vol. 43, No. 2, pg. 317.

First African Baptist Church, dedicated in 1884.

"A Choir of the Whole":
Black Baptist Churches of
Charlottesville & Albemarle County

"Faith of our fathers! Living still,
In spite of dungeon, fire, and sword;"
– Frederick W. Faber, 1814-1863

I t was a seemingly average Sunday in Charlottesville, much like
any other Sabbath, but the sounds emanating from the basement
of the three-story Delavan Hotel* marked it as something very special
indeed. Loud singing, hand-clapping, and shouting seeped out of the
building on the south side of West Main Street—past its heavy pillars
and the Albemarle clay-colored walls that surrounded it—
encompassing the entire block. The rhythmic stomping of feet could
also be heard and, at times, many dozens of voices in a fervent "Amen!"

A joyous noise it most certainly was for the passersby, but it's
doubtful whether any of them registered surprise, especially considering
the building's wonderful history. Named for Edward C. Delavan, an
upstate New York temperance leader, it was built in 1828 by Gen.
John Hartwell Cocke as an anti-alcohol boardinghouse for University
of Virginia students, the very first such. In the more than three dozen
years since, the Delavan had served as the home for several different
classical boarding schools, a hospital during the Civil War, the site of
Charlottesville's first mixed-race political meeting, and—in the

* *Note that a variant spelling, "Delevan," is currently in common use.*

57

immediate aftermath of the Civil War—the location of the area's first school for black children.[1]

True to form, that beautiful Sunday morning in 1867—or possibly early 1868, unfortunately no one recorded the exact date— the Delavan Hotel took part in another Charlottesville "first." That day it became the Delavan Church, and on that occasion it witnessed the first city gathering of a free black congregation in its own, independent setting. For the faithful black Baptists of central Virginia it had been a long, long journey.

With the end of the nation's bloody Civil War, black Baptist churches sprang up all across Virginia. Charlottesville and Albemarle County's participation in this liberating revival is, perhaps, best exemplified in the formation of three: First Baptist Church on West Main Street, Mount Zion Baptist Church on Ridge Street, and Union Run Baptist Church in Shadwell (near the birthplace of Thomas Jefferson). To the first congregations, the very establishment of these churches was their first step toward independence. Their voices, lifted loudly and proudly in both prayer and song, were finally being heard.

A few black Baptist churches had been in existence in the South prior to the Civil War. Historian William E. Montgomery, for example, wrote of the possible existence, in 1758, "of a black Baptist congregation on the plantation of William Byrd III on the Bluestone River in Virginia. . . ."[2] Black preachers who had been converted by itinerant missionaries in Georgia established a Baptist church near Savannah in 1773. It was constructed under the patronage of a wealthy white slaveholder. Seven years later, a similarly sponsored African Baptist Church was formed in Williamsburg, Virginia. During this period—it must be remembered—the religious education of enslaved people was generally frowned upon for fear of insurrection. An unwritten law, too, held that slaves should not be converted because Christians could not be kept in bondage.[3] Later, Christians cited the Biblical "curse of Ham" as the supposed reason blacks were forever doomed to serve white masters.[4]

In the Old Dominion a plethora of written laws successfully stifled antebellum religious enlightenment for African Americans. An 1804 law prohibited slaves from assembling after dusk for any purpose whatsoever. This was slightly amended the next year to allow bondsmen to attend religious services if they were in the company of their owners.[5]

Even the free black community—in Albemarle County usually about four percent of the total black population—was restricted. In 1832, for example, it was made illegal in Virginia for free blacks to preach, day or night, and sixteen years later they were prohibited from gathering at all. That same year, 1848, Virginia passed a law stating that only religious services presided over by white ministers would be considered lawful.[6]

The cumulative result of these regulations was that no separate Negro churches were established in Virginia until after the Emancipation Proclamation went into effect in 1863. Pre-emancipation black worship in Albemarle County, wrote Rosanna Liebman and Matilda McQuaid, "might then be described as an 'invisible institution' with no <u>outward</u> sign of independence from the white Baptist church."[7] Many local slaves nonetheless attended religious services—even some conducted by black preachers—in instances where sympathetic slave owners, and sympathetic white ministers, simply looked the other way. Secret gatherings, too—held in dimly lit slave quarters—were not uncommon. "It was here," penned Liebman and McQuaid, "that their independence began."[8]

In little Charlottesville, Virginia, the business of constructing churches got underway rather late—over sixty years after the founding of the town in 1762. "It was not until 1826, when the Christ Episcopal Church was completed," wrote Dr. Richard I. McKinney, "that there was a building for worship. . . . Prior to that date, the four major denominations [Methodist, Baptist, Presbyterian, and Episcopalian] held their services in the County Court House, each of the four having a designated Sunday in the month for their service."[9] By 1850, however, Charlottesville and Albemarle County could boast forty-five houses of worship seating a total of some 14,000 parishioners.

The First Baptist Church (white), on Park Street, wrote McKinney, "was formally organized in 1831, with Reuben L. Coleman, a student at the University of Virginia, as Pastor."[10] Serving in that capacity for six years, Pastor Coleman got the institution off to a good start, and the white congregation grew. So, too, did the number of the church's black adherents. In fact, all across Virginia— in the decades before the Civil War—an increasing number of blacks, both free and enslaved, became Baptists. According to McKinney, by 1854, the Baptist churches in Virginia were preaching God's word to "45,000 colored communicants. . . ."[11]

Why did such numbers flock to the Baptist faith when many of the largest slaveholders were Methodists, Presbyterians, and Episcopalians? "Many blacks," wrote Montgomery, "were Baptists for reasons entirely apart from the religious convictions of the significant whites in their lives. . . . Baptist theology [for one] blended particularly well with African religious traditions. The Baptists' insistence on baptism by immersion . . . resembled some of the river ceremonies common in areas of West Africa where many slaves had come from. More important, Baptist policy attracted blacks who wanted independence from white control. The principle of congregationalism [wherein the parishioners voted, democratically, over church matters] allowed for the accommodation of a wide range of beliefs and practices."[12]

Quite naturally, these Baptist traditions were also attractive to the black worshipers at First Baptist Church (white) on Park Street in Charlottesville. As the Civil War dragged on they grew increasingly unhappy with their segregated status in the church. They were being forced to listen to services from the balcony, had no voice in church affairs, and "in all probability," noted McKinney, "were treated more or less as the 'step children' of the congregation. . . ."[13] The issuance of the Emancipation Proclamation—which took effect on January 1, 1863—spurred them to action.

On March 16, 1863—only two and one half months later—the black members of the church, numbering an estimated 800 individuals, made an application to the church's pastor, the Reverend John T. Randolph, to form their own separate organization. Despite the intimidating fact that they were still living within the confines of the Confederacy—and the debilitating confines, of course, of the hideous institution of slavery—these brave souls were striking out for freedom. It seems highly likely that several of the church's free black members were among the leaders of this effort.[14]

At the next regular church meeting a committee put together to "ascertain the exact proposal" reported as follows: "The colored members . . . respectfully ask of their brethren,

> (1) That they, with the sanction of said brethren, obtain a place of worship for themselves to be held in trust for their use.
> (2) That, henceforth they may be allowed to select their own Pastor, Deacons, Clerk, Treasurer, and their delegates to the various Associations & in which they may obtain representation.
> (3) That, they may have the right to decide all matters of membership and discipline according to Baptist usage: and in general to be independent of the White church. . . .
> (4) That, they be allowed to select the trustees to hold the property for them, with the understanding that the said trustees shall be the white members of the Charlottesville Baptist Church."[15]

Perhaps not surprisingly, the church committee recommended that the "petition be granted with the understanding that all [delegates from the new institution to Baptist Associations] be white members of this Church."[16] And the secession movement continued forward, but not without the clearing-up of a few important details. A small group of free blacks, for example—led by Fairfax Taylor who had purchased his own freedom—did not agree with all of the terms of the petition. They were particularly unhappy with the choice of pastor. After a July 8, 1864 meeting—one at which the dissenters were told that they must "take or reject the organization without any reference to the Pastor"—the brand new church became an uncontested separate institution.[17]

"At first the new organization worshipped in the parent church," wrote McKinney, "with Reverend John T. Randolph as their Pastor."[18] Later white ministers of this black Baptist congregation included the Scottish-born Reverend James H. Fife—who built "Oak Lawn" to the south of Charlottesville and after whom "Fifeville" is named—as well as the Reverend John Walker George, the Northern-born proprietor of a Charlottesville general store. The records, unfortunately, do not tell us how long each of these white reverends served, although Mr. George's association with the church ended in 1868.[19]

As noted above, sometime in 1867, or early 1868, the black Baptists began holding their services in the basement of the Delavan Hotel. There—within the welcoming brick walls of a structure that had already accommodated so much liberating reform—they first experienced true, physical separation from the white parent church. The congregation purchased the forty-year-old structure on August 20, 1868, during the pastorage of Reverend George.[20]

The Delavan building—also called the "Mudwall" because of the dark-colored stucco wall that enclosed it—was condemned and razed eight years later, in 1876. Construction of a new church at the same location was begun the following year. By that time, the black congregation was already enjoying the services of its third black pastor. William Gibbons, a lay preacher possessed of "dynamic force and zeal," had been the first, remaining approximately two years. His wife, Isabella Gibbons, was one of central Virginia's first black public school teachers.[21]

"The second pastor was a Reverend W. J. Barnett," penned McKinney, "a West African who had come to the United States under the auspices of a northern missionary society."[22] Historian A. A. Taylor referred to Barnett as an outstanding black minister, adding that "he easily fitted into the life of the Negro of this country as attested by the large number of churches he organized" in central Virginia.[23] During these two ministries, baptisms were conducted at Hartman's Mill (on the Old Scottsville Road), Cochran's Mill (in the waters of Meadow Creek), and in the Rivanna River at the Charlottesville Woolen Mills at the east end of Market Street. The congregation's third pastor, who took office in 1873, was the Reverend M. T. Lewis.[24]

The new brick church—at the corner of 7th and West Main Streets—was dedicated on January 2, 1884. The July 16, 1884, edition of the Charlottesville *Jeffersonian* reported as follows: "The First African Baptist Church of Charlottesville worshipped in the basement of their new church last Sunday. . . . Services were commenced about sunrise Sunday morning, and were continued during the day. . . . This church is to be congratulated upon the energy displayed under the most trying circumstances."[25]

A twentieth-century pastor concurred. "The members of the church actually built most of it," explained Dr. Bruce Aaron Beard, who in 1994 began his ministry at what today is known simply as the First Baptist Church. "They continued to work on the farms and plantations they had worked on as slaves, then they'd come down here and work all night long. It took them quite some time but the total cost only came to around $7,000."[26] The upper portion of the building, with seating for 550, was completed in 1887.

Mount Zion Baptist Church at 105 Ridge Street—which local historian Vera Via referred to as "the second colored Baptist church in Charlottesville"—was also formed in the wake of the Civil War.[27] The sources differ, however, as to how the congregation first came together. In January of 1884, the Charlottesville *Jeffersonian* quoted the Reverend Alexander Truatt as saying that "[s]ome years since quite a number seceded [from the Delavan Church] and organized what is now known as Mount Zion Church, with the Reverend Jesse Herndon as pastor and about 700 members." In contradiction, a Mr. Henry Cash—ex-clerk of Mount Zion—stated, at about the same period, that "his church did not pull out from Delavan, but the two were formed about the same time, when the Negroes were dismissed from the white churches, by their own request around the end of the war."[28]

A 1967 *Daily Progress* piece places the year of the church's formation at 1867. "It was organized in the midst of gigantic and multitudinous events," reads the unattributed piece. "Many changes were taking place in the social climate. Our founding fathers came out of the white church and began meeting from house to house. Brother Samuel White, who was a consecrated Christian man, offered his home as a permanent meeting place."[29] This arrangement was found sufficient for a number a years. "About 1875," wrote U.Va. architecture professor K. Edward Lay, "the members built a frame church on Ridge Street that they called the Mount Zion First African Baptist Church of Charlottesville. In 1883 the frame church was razed and by 1884 it was replaced with a brick edifice designed by George Wallace Spooner. . . ."[30] Living just south of Mount Zion on Ridge Street, architect George Wallace Spooner (1820-1904), designed and constructed a number of churches in the City of Charlottesville.[31]

"The walls of Mount Zion Church are nearly finished," noted the *Jeffersonian* on March 19, 1884, "and unless we have another 'spell of weather' the roof will be on in a few days. . . . The congregation expects to worship in the basement by early summer."[32] Constructed in the Gothic Revival style, Spooner's creation has been called "one of the grander black churches" in Charlottesville. The pipe organ, steeple, and large stained-glass windows were added in the 1890s.[33]

"The Baptist emphasis on preaching," wrote noted architect Milton L. Grigg (in a passage concerning the local design of late nineteenth-century churches), "required that the congregation be able to hear readily, therefore, the greatest number should be closely grouped around the center of worship. For this reason, rather than creating an extensive large room, a gallery was inserted. . . . [During this period] there was not an emphasis on a choir. This space now so prominent in the church, was created at a later period. . . . At first, however, the jubilant and responsive congregation became a choir of the whole."[34]

Indeed, the fascinating traits of pre-emancipation black Baptist worship—loud hand-clapping, rhythmic dancing, exuberant singing—were fervently retained when freedom came. Black Baptist services were, and are, intensely emotional proceedings. "As had been true for their African ancestors, folk worship brought them into contact with the spirit world, an experience that was understandably joyous and exciting in comparison to the drabness of their daily lives. The emotional power of worship services, conveyed by the mesmerizing sermons of the preacher . . . and the ecstatic behavior of individuals 'getting the spirit' was highly contagious."[35]

That Baptist contagion, of course, had also been spread all across central Virginia. "In the second year of peace [1867]," wrote Monticello historian Lucia Stanton, "some of the fourteen thousand newly freed slaves of Albemarle County decided the time was right to build a church and a school."[36] In order to get a piece of land for their project, the congregation—which had already been together for about two years—dispatched representatives to meet with Thomas Jefferson Randolph, "the largest landholder in their neighborhood, a man who had recently claimed many of them as property."[37]

Randolph, one of Thomas Jefferson's grandsons, magnanimously granted them an acre on the fringe of his Edgehill estate. The deed, however—dated November 11, 1867—was not without stipulations. "He retained the right, to dismiss an objectionable teacher as well as to take back the land 'if at any time a political assemblage is held upon the said parcel.'"[38]

"Our first pastor was the Reverend Robert Hughes," explained the Reverend Rickey White, senior pastor of Union Run Baptist, the church subsequently erected on the granted acreage. "Hughes's grave is on the land here."[39]

Born into slavery at Monticello in 1824—when Mr. Jefferson was still alive—Robert Hughes preached at Union Run for almost thirty years. His older brother, George, served the congregation as deacon. Their father, Wormley Hughes, born in 1781, had begun work at Monticello as a "door-yard servant." By applying himself, picking up skills as he went along, Wormley Hughes became Jefferson's principal gardener.

Like his slave father, Robert Hughes eventually became a man who planted seeds: the seeds of spiritual enlightenment. And like the parishioners of Union Run Baptist Church—nowadays located just east of Shadwell—the determined congregations of Mount Zion and First Baptist Churches picked themselves up out of the pit of slavery, and followed the teachings of their faith into a better tomorrow.

Postscript: Shorty after the completion of this piece, I attended a very special Monticello ceremony—one dedicating one of the plantation's slave cemeteries. I listened, riveted to the spot, while descendants of Thomas Jefferson's enslaved community read aloud the names from a list of the men, women, and children who had lived there in bondage between 1770 and 1827. Robert Hughes's name was the 312th.

Endnotes

1. McKinney, Richard I., *Keeping the Faith; A History of The First Baptist Church, 1863-1980, In Light of Its Times* (Charlottesville, 1981), pgs. 45-46. See also: Schulman, Gayle M., "Learning in the Charlottesville Freedman's School: the First Jefferson School," *The Magazine of Albemarle County History* (Charlottesville, 2007), Vol. 64, pg. 102.

2. Montgomery, William E., *Under Their Own Vine and Fig Tree; The African-American Church in the South, 1865-1900* (Baton Rouge, 1993), pg. 27.

3. Liebwan, Rosanna, & McQuaid, Matilda, "The Rise of the Black Baptist Church; A Study of Ten Black Baptist Churches in Albemarle County" (unpublished document, Albemarle Charlottesville Historical Society [ACHS], 1983), pg. 1.

4. From the Book of Genesis, it concerns Noah's drunkenness and the accompanying shameful act perpetrated by his son Ham, the father of Canaan. Noah then damns Ham. The story's original objective was the justification of the subjection of the Canaanites under the Israelites. In later centuries, however, "the curse of Ham" was interpreted by many as an explanation for black skin—they were "cursed"—as well as a justification for the enslavement of an entire race.

5. Liebwan & McQuaid, "The Rise of the Black Baptist Church," pg. 2.

6. Ibid.

7. Ibid., pg. 3.

8. Ibid.

9. McKinney, *Keeping the Faith*, pg. 35.

10. Ibid.

11. Ibid., pgs. 37-8. The numbers McKinney found in Lloyd, Hermoine E., "History of Public Education of the Negro in Virginia" (unpublished M.A. thesis, Howard University, 1936), pg. 12.

12. Montgomery, *Under Their Own Vine and Fig Tree*, pgs. 107-08.

13. McKinney, *Keeping the Faith*, pg. 38.

14. Ibid., pgs. 38-9.

15. Ibid., pgs. 39-40.

16. Ibid.

17. Ibid., pg. 42.

18. Ibid., pg. 44.

19. Ibid., 44-5.

20. Ibid., pgs. 44-5.

21. Ibid., pgs. 48-9.

22. Ibid., pg. 49.

23. Taylor, A. A., *The Negro in the Reconstruction of Virginia* (New York, 1969), pg. 188.

24. McKinney, *Keeping the Faith*, pg. 49.

25. Quoted in Via, Vera V., "Looking Back," Charlottesville *Daily Progress*, March 24, 1955.

26. Interview of Dr. Bruce Aaron Beard conducted October 4, 2001.

27. Via, Vera V., "Looking Back," Charlottesville *Daily Progress*, March 24, 1955.

28. Ibid.

29. Unattributed, "Mount Zion Baptist Church; A Century of Christian Service," Charlottesville *Daily Progress,* January 7, 1967.

30. Lay, K. Edward, *The Architecture of Jefferson Country; Charlottesville and Albemarle County, Virginia* (Charlottesville, 2000), pg. 239.

31. Ibid. pg. 229.

32. Via, Vera V., "Looking Back," Charlottesville *Daily Progress*, March 4, 1955.

33. Lay, *The Architecture of Jefferson Country*, pg. 239.

34. Quoted in McKinney, *Keeping the Faith*, pgs. 53-4.

35. Montgomery, *Under Their Own Vine and Fig Tree*, pg. 108.

36. Stanton, Lucia, *Free Some Day; The African-American Families of Monticello* (Charlottesville, 2000), pgs. 159-60.

37. Ibid., pg. 160.

38. Ibid.

39. Interview of Rev. Rickey White conducted October 8, 2001.

Benjamin Franklin Ficklin (1827 – 1871).
(Courtesy of the Virginia Military Institute Archives.)

Benjamin Franklin Ficklin:
Thrill-seeker Extraordinaire

The date was April 3, 1860—the place, St. Joseph, Missouri. The crowd had assembled early in the afternoon to witness the momentous occasion scheduled for 5 p.m. Under broad-brimmed hats they stood outside the flag- and bunting-covered railroad station debating how the event would change their lives. Change was what St. Joseph was all about. The town of one thousand had first prospered as a staging point for the Colorado gold rush of 1849. Just recently, St. Joseph had become the westernmost railroad depot in all the United States. It was also the easternmost stop for the dust-covered stagecoaches of the Central Overland, California and Pike's Peak Express Company. Quite simply, St. Joe, Missouri, was the gateway to the West.

Standing at the front of the large crowd was Albemarle County native Benjamin Franklin Ficklin, the express company's general superintendent. He was tall, thin, and rugged-looking, and seemed—at the moment—to be especially preoccupied with his pocket watch. As the appointed hour approached, and passed, his mood deteriorated from frustration to anger. Then came word that the train from Hannibal, Missouri, would be delayed by as much as two hours. His schedule was utterly ruined. Onto the platform fronting the throng stepped Mayor M. Jeff Thompson, a Virginian well-known for his speechifying. The brass band quickly quieted down. This new express mail service, Thompson told the crowd, was merely the predecessor of rail lines extending all the way to the Pacific Ocean. "Citizens of

St. Joseph," he concluded loudly, "I bid you give three cheers for the Pony Express; three cheers for the first overland passage of the United States Mail!"[1] Much yelling, back-slapping, and cigar-puffing ensued.

When the train finally pulled in—and, unfortunately, the accounts differ as to the exact time—the mail from the East Coast was taken off, locked into a specially designed *mochila* (or saddlebag), and thrown overtop a saddle strapped to a feisty bay mare. "It was [now] up to blood, nerve and muscle," printed the New York *Sun*, "to take up the burden where fire, steam and mechanical skill left off."[2] Onto the horse vaulted Johnson William "Billy" Richardson, a small man who had "sailed for years," claimed the St. Joseph *Weekly West*, "amid the snow and icebergs of the Northern ocean."[3] (Presumably, Superintendant Ficklin had reasoned that this was just the type of experience that prepared a man to risk his life—alone, on horseback—as he raced through Indian territory.)

As the shouting rose to a crescendo, Ficklin tossed the courier a twenty-five-cent coin.

"What's this for?" asked the startled Richardson.

"For you to buy a rope," growled the impatient Ficklin, "and hang yourself if you don't make the correct time!" A shout, a slap to the horse's flank, and the first Pony Express rider was off.[4]

Benjamin Franklin Ficklin lived a life beyond believability— beyond amazing. If something exciting was happening, he was there— if it involved risk, he took it. A contemporary maintained that Ficklin's escapades, in fact, were more thrilling than those depicted in James Fenimore Cooper's *Last of the Mohicans*.[5] He helped conceive and initiate the Pony Express, dodged shot and shell in one of the Civil War's most desperate assaults, ran the blockade for the beleaguered Southern Confederacy, briefly owned Thomas Jefferson's Monticello, and barely escaped death numerous times while operating business ventures across the rough-hewn American West. Possessed of an extremely restless and adventurous spirit, Ben Ficklin was a thrill-seeker extraordinaire.

Benjamin Franklin Ficklin was born on his family's Albemarle County farm—located between Greenwood and the Mechum's River—on December 18, 1827. When Ben was still young the family moved to the tiny town of Charlottesville. His father was the Reverend Benjamin Ficklin, a well-to-do property owner and magistrate. In the 1830s the elder Ficklin also operated a dry goods and grocery store at lot #18 on Main Street. Ben's older brother, Slaughter W. Ficklin—who later owned the 1,000-acre Belmont estate just south of town—was a partner in Farish, Ficklin & Co., a stagecoach enterprise that also held the local contract for the delivery of the U.S. Mail. Undoubtedly, experience in his brother's enterprise was the germ that later helped Ben conceive of his own business ventures. Little has been written of Ben's youth, unfortunately, but early on he must have demonstrated his unflappable self-reliance, and unquenchable thirst for adventure.[6]

In 1844 Ben's family shipped him off to the Virginia Military Institute in Lexington. His marks were low, but his pranks at the school have raised him, over the years, to the lofty heights of legendary status. He was, for example, fond of firing off rockets at "improper" times. One frigid night he took charge of the superintendant's boots—those belonging to Francis H. Smith—and buried them deep in the snow. On another occasion, Ficklin painted the superintendent's horse, Old Coley, red, with zebra-like white stripes.[7]

The straw that finally broke the superintendent's back was a shenanigan involving a twelve-pounder cannon. One evening a howitzer was left outside of the V.M.I. arsenal, with its muzzle pointed directly at the cadet barracks. Ficklin quietly snuck out of his room, loaded the cannon with black powder, and gamely set it off. The explosion lit up the drill field and startled awake the slumbering students. Brother rat Norbonne Berkeley—whose bed was beneath a window—later wrote that he awoke to find he was "literally covered with glass."[8] The rowdy Ficklin was ushered away from the institute unceremoniously, the superintendent writing the family that Ben "stood ipso facto dismissed, and would return forthwith to his home."[9]

But Albemarle County *was not* exciting enough for Benjamin Franklin Ficklin. And, after all, the year was 1846—war had just broken out with Mexico. Instead of returning home Ben volunteered for service. Here the trail of truth becomes murky. One source places Ficklin in the U.S. Army, another in a volunteer company from Richmond. Ficklin himself wrote that he "[f]ought through numerous battles in Mexico and [was] severely wounded, and left for dead on the field of battle. . . ."[10] His obituary in the Charlottesville *Chronicle*, however, stated that he "joined a company starting for Mexico as a corporal; but, owing to bad health, was not able to go out with them."[11] In either case, he eventually reappeared, back in Lexington, at the superintendent's office.

To his old nemesis, Smith, Ficklin brashly announced, "Colonel, I have come back to be a cadet again."

"Mr. Ficklin," answered the startled "Old Specs," author of *Smith's Algebra*, "I can't reinstate you; it's impossible."

"Well sir," blurted the determined youngster, "I am going to sit right here until you do."[12]

A compromise was eventually reached—one that involved a promise of good behavior—and Ben Ficklin was soon back in the classroom. And he was graduated, fourth from the bottom of his class, on July 4, 1849. Once he had his diploma in hand, Ficklin reportedly filed it on the tip of his bayonet and marched triumphantly out of the auditorium.[13] He briefly tried to settle down—teaching school for a while in Abingdon, Virginia—but "the lure of the West was too great."[14]

Benjamin Franklin Ficklin first moved to Alabama, where he worked in the overland hauling business. By the mid-1850s, however, he was out on the western plains in the employ of the massive freight line that eventually became known as "Russell, Majors & Waddell." William H. Russell was a man of many enterprises and much political pull. Alexander Majors had experience running freight for the U.S. Army. Together their huge operation of 6,000 teamsters and 45,000 oxen connected isolated trapping, trading, and mining camps (as well as military installations), with the westernmost outposts of civilization in Missouri and East Texas. Indian raids were a constant threat. Famed newspaper man Horace Greeley visited the firm's Fort Leavenworth, Kansas, depot and wrote: "Such acres of wagons; such pyramids of extra axletrees; such herds of oxen; such regiments of drivers and other employees! No one who does not see can realize how vast a business this is; nor how immense are its outlays as well as its revenue."[15]

Ficklin learned quite a bit as a route agent for this firm. "He familiarized himself with the country (the West)," printed the San Angelo, Texas, *Evening Standard*, "made the acquaintance of the Indians, proved himself a shrewd trader, and mixed freely with the military, particularly at Fort Leavenworth where Texas' hero, Albert Sidney Johnston, was in command."[16] (Johnston, an 1826 West Point graduate, had served as senior brigadier general in the Texas Army, and as secretary of war for the Republic of Texas. He later fought with distinction in the Mexican War.) Ben Ficklin had finally found his element.

In the spring of 1857, Ficklin "was serving on a government-sponsored expedition to survey a wagon road from South Pass in the Rocky Mountains to Salt Lake City in Utah Territory."[17] The Mormon War broke out that same year. When Brevet U.S. Brig. Gen. Albert Sidney Johnston led a column of Federal troops into Utah to quell the rebellious Mormons, Ficklin signed up as courier and scout. His indomitable will and courage made him just the man for this kind of work. By mid-winter the expedition had run into trouble at Fort Bridger. The weather was hard, and after the Mormons burned three of Johnston's supply trains the army's horses grew painfully thin due to lack of feed. The men, too, were put on short rations.

On December 7, 1857, Johnston dispatched Ficklin, along with a small escort, to locate a trapper's settlement where forage and food were reportedly available. The trip turned into a forty-one-day ordeal of blistering cold, mind-numbing depravation, and frequent skirmishes with the belligerent "Latter Day Saints." Ficklin eventually located the camp, purchased the much-needed supplies, and successfully delivered them to Johnston's force. All this he'd performed against the advice of veteran trappers, "who declared it was suicide to undertake the journey at that time of year."[18]

In early 1859 Ben Ficklin was back in Fort Leavenworth, Kansas. The riverside community, much like St. Joseph only thirty miles upstream on the Missouri, was bustling with western commerce. After the discovery of gold in the Pike's Peak region of Colorado in 1858, William H. Russell and John S. Jones had started up a line of stagecoaches that linked Leavenworth with the Rocky Mountains. It was known as the "Leavenworth & Pike's Peak Express." Ficklin was the route agent. "Each coach was drawn by four fine, Kentucky mules, which were changed every twelve to twenty miles," remembered passenger William Larimer. "The stage fare between the Missouri River and Denver was at first $150 but later $100 each way."[19] Perhaps Russell and Jones should have charged more, for the enterprise soon went bust.

Not to be outdone, the route was bought out by Russell, along with partners Majors and W. B. Waddell. The entrepreneurs soon purchased another line that ran from St. Joe to Salt Lake City and the two businesses were combined. When the Territorial Legislature of Kansas granted a charter to the new "Central Overland California and Pike's Peak Express Company" in May, 1860, the listed incorporators were Russell, Majors, Waddell, F. A. Bee, John S. Jones, and Benjamin Franklin Ficklin. Also included was Ficklin's V.M.I.

brother, W. W. Finney of Powhatan County, Virginia. In the reorganization of the company, Ficklin was retained as the superintendent for the Denver to Salt Lake City section of the run.[20]

The stretch under Ficklin's management was long, and it traversed a region well-known for its lawlessness. Even some of the express company men were corrupt. "Opportunistic company employees were in cahoots with thieves and rustlers," penned David Maurer, "who were systematically emptying the company's corrals and stock pens."[21] At California Crossing, an immigrant ford of the South Platte, a vile French Canadian by the name of Jules Reni had established a settlement called Julesburg. Reni was also Ficklin's station-keeper for the Julesburg stopover. When Ficklin discovered that Reni was stealing from the company, he sent out Joseph Alfred "Jack" Slade to fire him. (A famed shootist, Slade was a Mexican War veteran who was in the employ of the express company as a division superintendent.)

Hiding in ambush, Reni greeted Slade with a blast from his shotgun (which luckily proved to be non-fatal). Ficklin, along with several well-armed men, arrived by the next coach and unceremoniously hanged Reni from the nearest available branch. Unfortunately, Ficklin didn't wait for the scoundrel to die, but instead headed off to the next station in order to stay on schedule. Reni's friends cut him down and took him into the hills to recover. There he was eventually captured and killed by Slade, who, without hesitating, lopped-off Reni's ears and attached one to his watch chain.[22]

Like father, like son—creations often take on the attributes of their creators. Ficklin and the rapid, but ultra-risky, mail-delivery enterprise that he next managed are both hazy with the fantastical embellishments of Western lore. Considered realistically, however, the Pony Express seems the natural extension of Ben Ficklin's talents, experiences, and thrill-seeking personality.

The Pony Express was undertaken as part of the huge, Central Overland California and Pike's Peak Express Company operation. Many authorities on the West maintain that Benjamin Franklin Ficklin, in fact, first hatched the idea. In the fall of 1854, Ficklin had accompanied newly elected California Senator William Gwin on part of his ride back to the national capital. (Gwin was a member of Congress's Post Office and Roads Committee, representing an entire state clamoring for the faster transport of the U.S. Mail.) It was upon this journey, wrote Colorado historian Le Roy R. Hafen, that "the scheme for a fast overland express was discussed." Gwin, in his memoirs, credited Ben Ficklin as the man "who originated the scheme [of the Pony Express] and carried it into operation."[23]

The plan for the Pony Express was nothing less that audacious. Originally the U.S. Mail traveled to the Pacific Coast via first the Gulf of Mexico, across the Isthmus of Panama, and by water again to the ports of California and the Oregon Territory. This trip, of course, took several months. As the pioneers reached further across the West, an overland mail route began to look feasible. William H. Russell, and his partners, were the first to attempt it. Russell announced the plan on January 27, 1860, and Ben Ficklin—as general superintendent of the new Pony Express—set out to make it a reality. He took on the massive task with a passion. By April 3 of the same year 190 relay stations were ready and manned. They stretched all the way from St. Joseph, Missouri to Sacramento, California—a total distance of 1,966 miles. Much of the line was over treacherous mountainous terrain, or across sun-baked desert sands. It also ran through Indian country.[24]

As part of his job Ficklin purchased 500 of the best blooded horses: he hired eighty experienced riders. They had to be young, fearless, and weigh under 125 pounds. The San Francisco newspaper ad announcing the undertaking read: "Wanted—young, skinny, wiry fellows not over 18. Must be expert riders, willing to risk death daily. Orphans preferred."[25] At the Fort Leavenworth office Alexander

Majors gave each of the "Pony" riders a Bible and made them sign a pledge that they would not "use profane language," drink "intoxicating liquors," or "quarrel or fight with any other employee of the firm."[26]

The best description of a "fast mail" Pony Express rider comes from the pen of Mark Twain: "Here he comes! . . . Away across the endless dead level of the prairie a black speck appears against the sky and it is plain that it moves. Well, I should think so. In a second or two it becomes a horse and rider, rising and falling, rising and falling—sweeping towards us, nearer and nearer—growing more and more distinct, more and more sharply defined—nearer and nearer, and the flutter of the hoofs comes faintly to the ear—another instant . . . a man and a horse burst past our excited faces, and go winging away like a belated fragment of a storm!"[27]

Perhaps surprisingly, the Pony Express remained in business only nineteen months. Despite this fact, the speed of the operation—Russell initially announced a schedule of thirteen days between New York and California—and the threat of Indian attack immediately captured the fancy of the newspaper-reading public. "Bob Haslam, muscular and square-jawed, was assigned to the worst of the Indian district through Nevada," wrote historian Arthur Chapman. Once, during the Pah-Ute Indian War, "Pony Bob" successfully completed a round-trip mail-run of 380 miles past relay stations that had been raided and burned out. Chapman wrote that Haslam was in the saddle thirty-six hours, "with danger threatening him in every canyon and at every turn of the trail."[28] The record for speed was set in March of 1861 when President Abraham Lincoln's inaugural address was carried to the Pacific Coast in seven days, seventeen hours.

Unfortunately, Ficklin only remained with the Pony Express until July of 1860. That month petty jealousies got the best of William Russell when he sent a telegram to the St. Joseph Pony Express office questioning Ficklin's loyalty. Outraged, Ficklin shot one back reading: "Send a man for my place damn quick!" He spent the better part of the next year, with partners Hiram Sibley and Jeptha Wade, in establishing the Pacific Telegraph Co. When completed on October 24, 1861, this endeavour completely outstripped the delivery speed of the Pony Express and put it out of business.[29]

In the spring of 1861 Ficklin once again heard the call of adventure, this time from the Old Dominion. When the Civil War began, Ficklin returned to Virginia and offered his services to his home state. On May 5, 1861, he was commissioned major and appointed temporary quartermaster general of the Provisional Army of the State of Virginia. His immediate superior was Gen. Robert E. Lee. But no desk job could hold the likes of Benjamin Franklin Ficklin—certainly not for long. When a Union army under Gen. George B. McClellan approached Richmond in May of 1862, Ficklin joined the Confederate forces in the field. On July 1 he participated in the disastrous Confederate assault at Malvern Hill, southeast of Richmond. There, according to Charlottesville editor James Alexander, Ficklin "succeeded by his own hands in saving a cannon abandoned by those who had served it."[30]

But army life, between battles, was notoriously dull. Lured by adventure on the high seas Ficklin soon thereafter became a blockade runner, operating three ships in that risky business: the *Virginia*, the *Coquette*, and the *Giraffe*. While in Europe between runs through the U.S. Navy's blockade, Ficklin often operated as a special purchasing agent for the Confederate government in Richmond. As such, in January of 1863, Ficklin was embroiled in controversy when he accused another blockade agent of "robbing the Confederate Government in a most shameful manner," a claim he was later forced to retract because he lacked proof.[31] Nonetheless, Ficklin's ocean-going operation must have netted him lots of cash. On November 17, 1864, he purchased Thomas Jefferson's Monticello, and 600 surrounding acres, from the Confederate Government for $80,500 in Southern currency. (The property had been confiscated as alien property by the C.S.A. in 1862.) Perhaps Ficklin dreamed of settling down next to his hometown, on land that adjoined his brother's Belmont estate.

In April of 1865 Benjamin Franklin Ficklin was in Washington D.C. Not surprisingly, perhaps, his purpose there is shrouded in mystery. One source claims he was involved in a cotton deal with Mrs. Lincoln's widowed sister, Mrs. Ben Hardin Helm. Another says he was on a secret peace mission attempting to gain an audience with the president himself.[32] On April 16—two days after Abraham Lincoln was shot—Ben Ficklin was arrested on the suspicion of his involvement in the assassination. An alert, and overly nervous, telegraph operator had reported him to the authorities. The man described the thirty-eight-year-old Ficklin as having "dark hair, cut short, sallow complexion, long thin nose," and "small black eyes." As a whole, he wrote, the six-foot-tall Ficklin presented "the appearance of a refined pirate."[33] Eventually, several of his Northern friends convinced the government that Ficklin had not been a part of the conspiracy, and he was released after spending a couple of months in prison.

Within two years he was back out west, running the U.S. Mail between San Antonio and El Paso. "Mr. Ficklin is an old stage man over the Salt Lake route and understands the business perfectly," printed the San Antonio *Express* in the fall of 1867, "he is also able to carry out all he assumes to do."[34] When his stagecoaches began suffering attacks from the pesky Kickapoo Indians, Ficklin acquired a U.S. Cavalry escort. He later armed his passengers with Spencer repeating carbines. But despite Indian attacks, rough terrain, and malevolent weather the mail and freight got through—as long as Ben Ficklin was in charge.[35] (In 1875 one of his western Texas stopovers was renamed Ben Ficklin in his honor. Unfortunately the town was washed away in the flood of August 24, 1882.)[36]

How does a life like Ficklin's end? Tortured to death by western ruffians? Gunned down in the street by a business rival? Eaten alive by a mountain lion? Benjamin Franklin Ficklin died on March 10, 1871. A jagged fishbone had lodged in his throat while he was dining at the Willard Hotel in Washington D.C. When a physician tried to remove it he unfortunately severed an artery and Ficklin drowned in his own blood. He was buried in Charlottesville's Maplewood Cemetery.

"Take his character throughout," noted the Charlottesville *Chronicle*, "and he was one of whom his mother State may well be proud. Brave, adventurous, kind-hearted and generous, he had at the same time gifts of intellect which made him the foremost man in every enterprise in which he was engaged."[37] The Honorable F. Lawley told the *London Standard* in 1895: "[A]fter listening to [Ficklin] for a couple of hours, you could not help being ashamed of yourself for having only the tame and prosaic life of civilization, which has in it nothing of the peril and 'snap' and still less of the camaraderie of frontier warfare."[38]

[Note: The author presents this piece at what he understands to be an immense risk to his future believability.]

Endnotes

1. Chapman, Arthur, *The Pony Express; The Record of a Romantic Adventure in Business* (New York, 1932), pg. 105.

2. Ibid., pg. 104.

3. Ibid., pg. 107.

4. Uncredited newspaper piece, "Ben Ficklin Now Credited With Pony Express Origin," San Angelo, Texas, *Evening Standard*, April 29, 1948. See also: Maurer, David A., "Pony Express Pioneer Left His Mark on VMI," *VMI Alumni Review* (Lexington, 1993), Vol. 69, No. 4, pg. 2 for another version of this account. Note that Maurer names Johnnie Frey, rather than "Billy" Richardson, as the first Pony Express rider. See, however: Hafen, Le Roy R., *The Overland Mail, 1849-1869; Promoter of Settlement, Precursor of Railroads* (Cleveland, 1926), pg. 172. He writes that Louise Platt Hauck, in her article, "The Pony Express Celebration," *Missouri Historical Review*, Vol. xvii, pg. 437, considered the many varying claims, and "seems to have settled the dispute in favor of Johnson William Richardson."

5. "Ben Ficklin," San Angelo, Texas, *Evening Standard*, April 29, 1948.

6. Maurer, "Pony Express Pioneer," pg. 2; Rawlings, Mary, ed., *Early Charlottesville; Recollections of James Alexander, 1828-1874* (Charlottesville, 1942), pgs. 30 & 72. Accounts differ as to Ficklin's date of birth. The earlier accounts—such as the Charlottesville *Chronicle* piece of March 17, 1871—say he was born on December 18, not the 28.

7. "Ben Ficklin," San Angelo, Texas, *Evening Standard*, April 29, 1948.

8. Read, B. M., "Ben Ficklin 1849 and the Pony Express," *VMI Alumni Review* (Lexington, summer 1973), pg. 13.

9. Ibid.

10. Ibid., pg. 14.

11. Charlottesville *Chronicle*, March 17, 1871.

12. Read, "Ben Ficklin," pg. 14.

13. "Ben Ficklin," San Angelo, Texas, *Evening Standard*, April 29, 1948.

14. Read, "Ben Ficklin," pg. 14.

15. Chapman, *The Pony Express*, pg. 237.

16. "Ben Ficklin," San Angelo, Texas, *Evening Standard*, April 29, 1948.

17. Austerman, Wayne R., *Sharps Rifles and Spanish Mules; The San Antonio-El Paso Mail, 1851-1881* (College Station, Texas, 1985), pg. 207.

18. "Ben Ficklin," San Angelo, Texas, *Evening Standard*, April 29, 1948.

19. Chapman, *The Pony Express*, pg. 78.

20. Ibid., pgs. 78-9.

21. Maurer, "Pony Express Pioneer," pg. 5.

22. Ibid. A famous part of Western lore, this story has numerous variations. Reni, for example, is sometimes referred to as "Beni." See also: http://www.xphomestation.com/bficklin.html.

23. Hafen, *The Overland Mail*, pg. 165.

24. Chapman, *The Pony Express*, pg. 84.

25. Read, "Ben Ficklin," pg. 14. This famous ad can be found in most any Pony Express write-up. Note that one modern-day historian claims that the ad is a twentieth-century fabrication.

26. Chapman, *The Pony Express*, pg. 98.

27. Twain, Mark, *Roughing It* (Hartford, 1872), pg. 54.

28. Chapman, *The Pony Express*, pgs. 121 & 218.

29. Maurer, "Pony Express Pioneer," pg. 6.

30. Charlottesville *Chronicle*, March 17, 1871. This claim is perhaps made more believable by the fact that, at the Battle of Malvern Hill, numerous Confederate artillery pieces were abandoned by their crews due to the overwhelming superiority there of the Federal guns.

31. Vandiver, Frank E., *Ploughshares Into Swords; Josiah Gorgas and Confederate Ordnance* (Austin, 1952), pgs. 90 & 95.

32. See Charlottesville *Daily Progress*, January 17, 1987, letter to the editor titled "McLean Man Seeks Ficklin Information," and Maurer, "Pony Express Pioneer," pg. 7.

33. Maurer, "Pony Express Pioneer," pg. 7.

34. San Antonio *Express*, September 30, 1867.

35. Austerman, *Sharps Rifles and Spanish Mules*, pgs. 210-40..

36. "Ben Ficklin," San Angelo, Texas, *Evening Standard*, April 29, 1948.

37. Charlottesville *Chronicle*, March 17, 1871.

38. "Ben Ficklin," San Angelo, Texas, *Evening Standard*, April 29, 1948.

The Rotunda at the University of Virginia, October 27, 1895.
(Photo by Rufus W. Holsinger.)

"A Most Fearful Calamity": The 1895 U.Va. Rotunda Fire[1]

It was a bright, cool autumn morning. Tucked into a small office inside the Staunton C. & O. Railroad Station, the telegraph dispatcher lounged with his feet up, the Sunday edition of the *Spectator* sprawled across his lap and overtop his huge oak desk. The Bunnel "Sideswiper" Telegraph rested quietly beneath an unread spread of newsprint. Sharp, clean light penetrated the room through an open door leading out onto the platform. Just outside a pair of lads in gabardine sailor suits attempted to carve their initials into a well-worn bench. The date was October 27, 1895.

Suddenly the Bunnell sounder began spitting out the clunks and clicks of an urgent message from Charlottesville. The newspaper flew to all corners as the operator quickly translated the stunning communication: "University on fire: beyond our control: water out: send fire department."[2]

"Hey you—you boys there," shouted the man frantically, "run down to the fire company and tell the captain to sound the alarm! Mr. Jefferson's University is on fire!"[3]

The 1895 Rotunda fire was a tremendous shock to the University of Virginia community and Charlottesville. U.Va.-born journalist Virginius Dabney called it "a catastrophe of the first magnitude."[4] Students, faculty, and firefighters battled the blaze for several hours, during which time heroism became commonplace, but, eventually, they yielded to the inevitable. The centerpiece of

Thomas Jefferson's "academical village"—perhaps his most palpable central Virginia legacy—was gutted. Historian Philip Alexander Bruce wrote that the conflagration "was so sudden, so unexpected, so startling in its occurrence; so destructive in its physical consequences; so far reaching in its moral influence—that it can, with perfect accuracy, be taken as a milestone to mark the close of one period and the opening of another."[5]

The University of Virginia Rotunda is one of Jefferson's most wonderful creations, and, according to modern architects, one of the most beautiful buildings in all the United States. The idea of organizing his University around an architecturally dominant building, however, was most likely not his. In 1817—when Jefferson was casting about for physical plans for what was then "Central College"—he wrote to Benjamin Henry Latrobe for suggestions. At that time the fifty-three-year-old English-born architect was in Washington, working on the south wing of the U.S. Capitol. Latrobe dashed off several sketches. One included a round central building which, he wrote, "ought to exhibit in mass and details as perfect a specimen of good architectural taste as can be devised."[6] The thumbnail drawing, in fact, closely resembles Jefferson's final design.

Work on the Rotunda began on October 7, 1822. For additional guidance the ex-president had re-consulted Andrea Palladio, the sixteenth-century Italian architect whose sketchbooks had inspired Monticello. Using a copy of Giacomo Leoni's 1721 edition of Palladio's *Four Books of Architecture*, Jefferson modeled the cylindrical building after the Pantheon in Rome. Jefferson scaled down his Rotunda, however, to a diameter of seventy-seven feet, "being one-half that of the Pantheon, consequently [having] one-fourth its area and one-eight its volume."[7] The first two floors were designed as meeting halls and classrooms. The dome room on the upper level was created as the school's library; thus placing the handsome structure at the intellectual center of all the institution's functions. Jefferson personally wrote out a list of 6,900 volumes that he intended as the University's first collection.[8]

Prior to its completion the Rotunda witnessed a memorable occasion. On November 5, 1824, the Marquis de Lafayette—who was in Virginia during his "Triumphal Tour" of the United States—was honored by the citizens of Albemarle County with a special banquet in the dome room. Four hundred individuals were seated in three concentric circles. As good cheer and toasts resounded across the circular hall, Thomas Jefferson handed a brief commemorative speech to V. W. Southall. "[Lafayette's] deeds in the war of independence you have heard," read the gentleman on behalf of the "Father of the University," "[h]is deeds, in the peace which followed that war, are perhaps not known to you, but I can attest them. When I was stationed in his country . . . [Lafayette] was my most powerful auxiliary and advocate. . . . In truth, I only held the nail, he drove it."[9] The Marquis was so moved by his old friend's tribute that he stood, grabbed Jefferson by the hand, and wept out loud.

Thomas Jefferson last visited the Rotunda in June of 1826. On his horse Eagle he rode down from the "little mountain." The eighty-three-year-old climbed the Rotunda stairs and, from the vantage point of his own creation, watched for an hour while workmen carefully placed an Italian-made Corinthian capital. The Rotunda was finally completed in September of that year, but, unfortunately, the "Sage of Monticello" had died two months earlier on July 4, the fiftieth anniversary of the adoption of the Declaration of Independence.

Soon after opening its doors in 1825 the University of Virginia became the preeminent southern institution of higher learning. Enrollment—from the initial year's total of 116—grew so steadily that by 1849, according to Professor of Architecture Frederick Doveton Nichols, the institution was suffering from the lack of two vital necessities. The first of these was water, but the more serious at the time seemed to be classroom space. The following year, in fact, the faculty complained that only two schools—Natural Philosophy and Chemistry—enjoyed the use of their own classrooms. The five additional disciplines, they reported, were suffered to share two other lecture halls.[10]

In September of 1850, therefore, the accomplished architect Robert Mills was selected to design another building. To the later disgust of many, including the founder's grandson Thomas Jefferson Randolph, Mills and the University rector came up with a plan to attach a wing, an annex, to the Rotunda's north portico. Completed in 1852, at the cost of $35,000, the hideous addition was one hundred feet long and fifty-four feet wide. But, at least, it temporarily solved the problem of space. Connected to the Rotunda by means of a thirty-foot-long wooden portico, the Annex featured classrooms on the first and third floors, as well as in the basement. The second story was one large auditorium that could accommodate twelve hundred. In 1857 the rear of the speaker's platform was graced with a Paul Balze copy of Raphael's *School of Athens*, a fitting reminder of Jefferson's admiration for the Greek practices of education.

To address the lack of water, a civil engineer was employed by the University in 1855. Using iron pipes he connected a reservoir behind the Rotunda with several springs to the west. "From the reservoir, the water was forced up by steam pump into two tanks located within the base of the dome of the Rotunda."[11] This system proved inadequate, however, during a small fire in the spring of 1861. That flare-up in the Rotunda was quickly put out by the students. Perhaps, after this near disaster, the administration was lulled into assuming that large gangs of volunteers would squelch any threatening blaze. If this was indeed their line of reasoning, they were sadly mistaken.

Sunday, October 27, 1895, began as a typically beautiful autumn day. The sky was clear and the hint of coolness only added a bit of spring to the step. Shortly after 10:00 a.m. a student by the name of Foshee noticed smoke issuing from the ventilator in the cornice of the Annex's northern facade. His shouts quickly brought over two others and the three immediately bolted toward the bell tower to alert Henry Martin. Sixty-nine-year-old "Uncle" Henry— an ex-slave who claimed his mother had been owned by Mr.

Jefferson—leapt to the rope and sounded the tocsin while the young gentlemen ran to the engine-house.[12] The bell's first clangs were taken as the call for morning service, but, according to Philip Bruce, "the prolonged ringing, followed by loud cries of fire, caused the young men to swarm out of their dormitories and rush down the arcades and up the Lawn to the Rotunda."[13] "Everyone was running to the Rotunda," wrote student John T. Thornton to his mother, "and soon a large crowd was assembled."[14] Also quick on the scene was William H. Echols who, aside from his professorial duties, was also in charge of buildings and grounds. Virginius Dabney described "Reddy" Echols as "a magnificently masculine, broad-shouldered, red-haired man of about six feet four, [who] was utterly fearless."[15] That quality was about to be tested.

Margaret Taylor Randolph, one of Jefferson's great granddaughters, was entering a church on West Main Street when she first heard of the fire. As she joined the congregation, "Mr. Lee [the pastor] was just saying, 'Let us pray that our great seat of education may not be entirely destroyed by fire.'" A Mrs. Kirk remembered that the church windows were covered in order to hide the disturbing spectacle to the west. Evidently the effort was not enough. "After the prayer," wrote Randolph, "I went to the window and there saw a tall blaze coming out of the north corner of the roof over the [Annex]."[16]

Morgan Poitiaux Robinson and several other students were lounging at No. 33 West Range when they heard the "shouting of those hurrying to get to the [fire] engine . . . mingled with the chopping of an axe (cutting open the engine-house door) and the cry of 'Fire!'"[17] In mere moments they found themselves hauling the small engine and hose-reels to the edge of the pond (near the site of the present-day chapel). While Professor R. C. Minor supervised, they rapidly ran off an extended line of hose. But, unable to draw from the pond because the engine faulted a suction pipe, one end had to be dragged to a water plug near Madison Hall. Meanwhile the other end was boldly advanced up the high narrow backstairs leading to the rear door of the stage in the Annex's "Public Hall" (or auditorium).

Once inside the auditorium, the student firefighters discovered that the blaze had begun in one of the Engineering Department rooms in the northwest corner of the Annex's top level. The public hall's ceiling was covered with billows of black smoke. The fire had already consumed much of the planking above and was lapping away at the left-hand corner of the *School of Athens*. Evidently the rush of air through a small flue was feeding the fire. (Philip Bruce later theorized that the fire must have originated in one of the following three areas: the space between the auditorium's ceiling and the floor of an upstairs instrument-room; a gap separating the lower and upper surfaces of an arch above the stage; or an enclosed space alongside this arch. The faculty reported that there had been problems with the lighting, so it's possible that defective wiring through one of these areas had cast a spark.[18])

A ladder was leaned against the huge painting and Professor Echols, along with several volunteers, hoisted the hose up the rungs to assault the flames. But they were already too high above the water-mains—which were rusty with age—and the stream from the nozzle was only five feet in length. It was woefully inadequate. Meanwhile the Annex's hallways and staircases were frenetic with activity as a throng of students attempted to save the Law Library books and the paraphernalia of the physical and mechanical laboratories. The flames were gaining on them, however, and many of the rooms were choked with overpowering fumes. Morgan Robinson remembered that when "the beam holding the lights and reflectors . . . came down to the stage with a crash, followed by a great shower of sparks and heavy burning brands," Professor Milton W. Humphries stated calmly: "Gentlemen, I think that we shall have to take up another line of defense."[19]

Professor Echols and University Conservator of the Peace J. A. Bishop, seeing that the Annex could not be saved, retreated under the portico joining it to Mr. Jefferson's beautiful Rotunda, his "sphere within a cylinder." Fortunately Bishop had brought along one hundred pounds of dynamite. Amid the flames, sky-blackening smoke, and confusion the two blasted away the four columns supporting the portico's roof structure. The fire could not be allowed to reach the Rotunda! Spectators reportedly threw rocks at these gentlemen while they were thus engaged, evidently thinking that they misunderstood their danger. The pillars soon fell with weighty thuds; but the roof did not.[20]

Without hesitation Echols and Bishop climbed up to the Rotunda's wooden dome to finish off the portico. From that vantage it was easy to see that time was running short. Deciding they needed more dynamite for the job they rushed back down to add to their arsenal. Dr. Gordon Wilson was quickly collared from the crowd and sent by buggy to the nearest general supply store. While he was away, "Prof. Echols and his associates made free use of the axes, which Uncle Henry had gotten . . . to cut down the door to the secret passageway leading up through the walls of the Rotunda to the dome. . . ."[21] This would serve as an additional exit if the flames should gut the building.

When Dr. Wilson returned, the dynamite was quickly packed into two-bushel meal bags, which had appeared—as if by magic—from the bystanders. Thus loaded down, Professor Echols and Mr. Bishop, with no thought whatsoever to their own safety, mounted the narrow stairs up the passageway to the dome. What an appalling scene they espied from the summit! Above the Annex rose a great dense plume, its underside brightly lit by wicked flames dancing on the roof-beams. And these wind-fanned demons were fast approaching. From below rose the shouts and commands of professors attempting to organize the masses. Hundreds of Sunday-dressed Charlottesvillians were assisting the small army of students running overloaded with books and apparatus; precious items that were now being retrieved from the threatened Rotunda. Several volunteers lay prostrate on the Lawn amid the piles of rescued objects. To this mayhem was soon added the sharp detonations of dynamite cartridges as Echols and Bishop tossed the lethal sticks at the thirty-foot-long portico roof. The sound waves from these explosions reverberated from the slopes of Monticello Mountain. One witness recorded that the blasts left "but two scantlings standing."[22] In reality, however, it was too little, too late. "They tried to blow up the Portico . . . in the hope that . . . the Rotunda might be saved," wrote John Thornton, "but all to no purpose."[23] The flames had already reached the dome.

Inside the Rotunda the effort was focused on saving the contents of the University's main library. "The boys worked like fiends," wrote Thornton.[24] "[A]ll was chaos and confusion," penned Robinson ten years after the fire, "the jingle of the glass being broken from the bookcases, the yells and shouts of those working to save the books, the orders of those who were directing the work of the rescue. . . ."[25] From the crowd now both men and women entered the burning cylinder and offered their assistance. "At first the men had tried to drive the women away, telling them that they would save all the books, etc., but they would not go, [and] worked everywhere the men worked—even in the bucket-lines."[26] Inside, the ladies stood by the bookshelves, vigorously helping to pile the volumes onto arms held extended. These would then be rushed over to the window above the Rotunda's south entrance and tossed out to anxious watchers below. Many of the precious tomes were caught in outstretched blankets. In this manner almost 12,000 of the institution's 57,000 books were spared. But there was much more that needed saving.

One student, caught up in the rush of excitement, picked up the marble bust of Law Professor John Barbee Minor and carried it down the stairs to the Lawn. He immediately returned to rescue its pedestal. Buoyed by this success, several students determined to save the splendid marble statue of Jefferson by Virginia-born sculptor

Alexander Galt. (In this piece, perhaps uncharacteristically, Jefferson wears a long flowing cloak.) Someone produced a rope and soon the stone image of the author of the Declaration had a noose around its neck. With the other end of the rope wound about an upstairs gallery pillar, the ex-president was carefully lowered onto a table. This immediately collapsed, chipping away a piece of the cloak's right-hand hem. Using the rope the students dragged Jefferson to the library's only exit—one which was, of course, completely jammed with people running in and out.

"It was an awful scene," wrote Morgan Robinson. "The roar of the flames which were now well in the room and cast a dull, red, fiendish glow over everything through the smoke; the crackling of burning embers; all these things tended to make [it] a veritable hell. . . ."[27] Suddenly there was a huge explosion that violently shook the structure. Every remaining pane of glass was shattered. All those inside believed they were doomed. "[W]ith a terrific crash the whole plaster ceiling of the dome of the Rotunda came down to the floor," remembered Robinson.[28] This gave incentive to a frantic rush to the exit. The momentum soon encouraged the statue down the stairs—feet foremost and ripping off the top of each riser. Once out on the South Portico, Mr. Jefferson was eased down the marble steps with the aid of mattresses. It had taken half a day and much equipment to position the Alexander Galt: removing it had been the work of but fifteen minutes.

Now it was certain that the Rotunda would be lost. Outside the crowd turned its attention to saving the adjacent pavilions. Wet blankets were hung over the wooden eaves. Bucket-brigades were formed to toss water over the nearest roofs and terraces. These lines were furnished with pitchers, basins, and every domestic object that could carry water. Luckily nature seemed to take an interest at this moment as a strong wind from the south helped prevent the fire from surging down the Lawn. "Reddy" Echols, Bishop, and a Mr. Finch dynamited the wings on either side of the Rotunda. While laying the charges Echols fell through a roof and broke his left hand. To the mass of humanity battling the fire was now added fifteen firefighters and engine No. 4 from the Staunton Volunteer Fire Company. They had received an urgent plea via telegraph. Help also arrived from Lynchburg aboard an especially commandeered train.

When the Rotunda became too dangerous, Col. Charles S. Venable barred the doors. Through the windows the inside appeared as one massive roaring furnace. "[T]he whole Rotunda was lit up from top to bottom," remembered Bell Dunnington, a faculty member's daughter.[29] "It was a magnificent sight . . . as the fresh air rushed in and cleared away the smoke," noted Robinson, you could see "the pillars in the gallery . . . [and] some dusty books left to their fate . . . [when] a perfect volcano of flame poured into the Rotunda from the Annex. . . ."[30] When the blaze finally reached the mechanism of the old Rotunda clock it froze—at five minutes to twelve. Eventually it fell back into the conflagration. At 1:00 p.m. the great dome of Mr. Jefferson's Rotunda collapsed and smashed through what was left of the floors below. With it fell the bronze bell Jefferson had ordered from Medway, Massachusetts, the year before he died. Hundreds of spectators wept.

"Poor old [Professor George Frederick] Holmes was walking without his hat on with tears rolling down his cheeks, picking up any stray piece of manuscript he came across. . . ." wrote Margaret Taylor the day of the fire.[31] "I love this old University with all my heart," John T. Thornton wrote at the same time, "and I who am comparatively young, am so grieved what must be the distress of those old professors who have worked for the University so long and lectured so often within those now ruined walls! . . . Misfortune after misfortune has crippled [the University's] usefulness and now this crowning blow, [that] this building planned and built by Jefferson, this splendid library, our so famous copy of the *School of Athens*, the dear old clock that never kept time, should be destroyed, seems to be the crowning evil and the worst that this nemesis who pursues us would let fall on our heads. Horrible! Horrible! Horrible!"[32]

But, of course, all was not lost, and the administration responded to its "distress" with an unshaken determination. "The ruins were still smoldering," wrote Virginius Dabney, "when the faculty met that [very] afternoon and resolved, despite the disaster, to carry on the work of the University."[33] Classes were held the next day, albeit in rearranged and makeshift lecture halls. And, within a short time, New York architect Stanford White was selected to reconstruct the burnt out Rotunda. Over the objections of a few, he rebuilt the interior in his classical-Renaissance "Beaux Arts" style. Thankfully, Jefferson's "sphere within a cylinder" was restored to its original design in time for the two-hundredth anniversary of its creator's Declaration of Independence.

"The catastrophe of 1895 was an appalling one," wrote historian Philip Bruce, "but the firm resolution with which it was faced, the practical wisdom with which it was redressed, [and] the outburst of filial loyalty and affection which it caused, left behind . . . a splendid tradition of sagacity, courage and devotion, which seemed, in its moral influence at least, to be almost a full compensation for the destructive physical consequences of that dreadful day."[34]

Endnotes

1. John T. Thornton to Rosalie Thornton, October 26 [27], 1895, quoted in Vaughan, Joseph Lee, and Gianniny, Omer Allan, Jr., *Thomas Jefferson's Rotunda Restored, 1973-76; A Pictorial Review With Commentary* (Charlottesville, 1981), pg. 23. A student at the time, John Thornton was the son of the chairman of the faculty, William Mynn Thornton. Young Thornton penned to his mother in Berlin: "I write to let you know of a most fearful calamity which has befallen the dear old University."

2. Robinson, Morgan Poitiaux, *The Burning of the Rotunda; Being a Sketch of the Partial Destruction of the University of Virginia (1895)* (Richmond, 1905), pgs. 19-20. Note that another version of this same booklet—with differing page numbers—was published in 1921.

3. While working at the *Richmond Times-Dispatch* as a broadcast journalist, I became enamored of "action ledes" as they're called in news journalism. As story introductions, they're designed to draw the reader in by putting them right into the middle of the action. This intro is fictitious, but it's based on information found mostly in Robinson, *The Burning of the Rotunda*, pgs. 3-20.

4. Dabney, Virginius, *Mr. Jefferson's University; A History* (Charlottesville, 1981), pg. 40. Born at U.Va. Hospital in 1901, Dabney's father, Richard Heath Dabney, was a U.Va. professor of history. Virginius Dabney was awarded a Pulitzer in 1948.

5 Bruce, Philip Alexander, *History of the University of Virginia, 1819-1919; The Lengthened Shadow of One Man* (New York, 1921), Vol. IV, pg. 252.

6. Bruce, *History of the University*, Vol. I, pg. 186.

7. Quoted in: Wills, Garry, *Mr. Jefferson's University* (Washington, D.C., 2002), pg. 112.

8. Hogan, Pendleton, *The Lawn; A Guide to Jefferson's University* (Charlottesville, 1987). This slender guidebook is filled with great information on the construction of the University.

9. Quoted in: Britton, Rick, *Jefferson; A Monticello Sampler* (Buena Vista, Va., 2008), pg. 157.

10. Nichols, Frederick Doveton, "A Day to Remember; The Burning of the Rotunda, 1895," *The Magazine of Albemarle County History* (MACH) (Charlottesville, 1959), Vol. XVII, pg. 57.

11. Ibid., pg. 60.

12. For a wonderful tribute to Henry Martin see: Patton, John S., and Doswell, Sallie J., *The University of Virginia; Glimpses of Its Past and Present* (Lynchburg, 1900), pg. 82.

13. Bruce, *History of the University*, Vol. IV, pg. 254.

14. Vaughan and Gianniny, *Thomas Jefferson's Rotunda Restored*, pgs. 23-5.

15. Dabney, *Mr. Jefferson's University*, pg. 40.

16. Nichols, "A Day to Remember," pg. 61.

17. Robinson, *The Burning of the Rotunda*, pg. 4.

18. Bruce, *History of the University*, Vol. VI, pgs. 255-56.

19. Robinson, *The Burning of the Rotunda*, pgs. 5-6.

20. Ibid., pgs. 6-7.

21. Ibid., pgs. 7-8.

22. Ibid., pg. 8.

23. Vaughan and Gianniny, *Thomas Jefferson's Rotunda Restored*, pg. 25.

24. Ibid.

25. Robinson, *The Burning of the Rotunda*, pg. 8.

26. Ibid., pg. 9.

27. Ibid., pg. 10.

28. Ibid., pg. 12.

29. Quoted in: Hogan, *The Lawn*, pg. 5.

30. Robinson, *The Burning of the Rotunda*, pg. 14.

31. Nichols, "A Day to Remember," pg. 62.

32. Vaughan and Gianniny, *Thomas Jefferson's Rotunda Restored*, pgs. 25-6.

33. Dabney, *Mr. Jefferson's University*, pg. 40.

34. Bruce, *History of the University*, Vol. VI, pg. 253.

A U.S. Army bell tent in use at C.C.C. Camp Roosevelt.
(Photo by United States Forestry Service.)

A "New Deal" in the Sky:
The CCC & the Building of the Skyline Drive

Oh, those beans, bacon, and gravy,
They almost drive me crazy,
I eat 'em till I see 'em in my dreams;
When I wake up in the morning,
And another day is dawning,
Yes, I know I'll have another mess of beans.
    – *Beans, Bacon, and Gravy*, (Refrain) 1932[1]

It was the worst of times; it was the worst of times.[2] Events moved so rapidly after October 24, 1929, that the nation was left dumbstruck. "Black Thursday's" crash shattered Wall Street's smug facade and exposed an understructure rotting of greed and foolish speculation. America's economy was left in ruins. Building construction came to a halt, factories cut production, and businesses cut salespeople. Within only two months several million Americans were out of work. Eventually the nationwide unemployment rate rose to an unfathomable twenty-five percent. The land of plenty had become the land of hunger. Harvard economist John Kenneth Galbraith has called the Great Depression that followed "the most momentous economic occurrence in the history of the United States."[3]

In the years immediately after the crash the financial blight spread into households all across the country. For many unfortunates, life-sustaining food became the daily obsession. Families that still had a wage-earner scrimped and made substitutions; others went without. The Depression's deepest wounds were borne by the country's

101

youth. "Years of poverty, hunger, and disillusionment piled a weight of suffering on shoulders too young to bear it," wrote Milton Meltzer.[4] Debilitating poverty drove many of these juveniles to leave home. They soon became known as America's "teenage tramps." By late 1932 a quarter of a million youngsters under the age of twenty-one were wandering the country looking for food, shelter, and work.[5] Virginians were no exception. But, in those days of gloom, one ray of hope appeared in March of 1933: President Franklin Delano Roosevelt announced plans to employ up to half a million of the nation's youth in the parks and national forests. The Civilian Conservation Corps was born.[6]

The Civilian Conservation Corps—also known as the CCC—came as a godsend to the dispossessed youth of central Virginia. Their homes had been shattered, their parents needed money, and their younger brothers and sisters were pale and thin. The invigorating outdoor work improved their health—the steady income helped stabilized their families. The CCC Camps in the Shenandoah National Park were among the first in the nation. Along Virginia's misty Blue Ridge, President Roosevelt's "tree army" found character-building work and a sense of belonging that many carried for the rest of their days.

The story of Shenandoah National Park's CCC Camps begins years before the crash of '29. As early as the turn of the century, federal officials had been considering the placement of a national park in the eastern region of the United States. Tennessee, Kentucky, North Carolina, and Virginia vied for the distinction and tourist dollars that a large park would generate. "Representatives from Kentucky lobbied for Mammoth Caves," wrote Andrew Myers, "North Carolina and Tennessee for the Great Smoky Mountains, and Virginia for the Blue Ridge."[7] Virginia Governor E. Lee Trinkle treated the competition as "an affair of honor," something that would reawaken "the great Virginia spirit."[8]

In December of 1924 a congressional task force called the "Southern Appalachian National Park Committee" recommended that the new park be established along Virginia's Blue Ridge Mountains. The question of property rights was problematic, they admitted, but the range's proximity to several large cities made it an ideal location. Committee members made the trek into the mountains and were particularly impressed by the stunning vistas of the Shenandoah Valley, Massanutten Mountain, and the patchwork-quilt counties of Page and Warren. Their report also mentioned the idea of a scenic roadway skimming the Blue Ridge crestline. It noted that a possible feature of the park would be a "skyline drive along the mountain top. . . . Few scenic drives in the world could surpass it."[9]

Landscape architects had been designing roads for pleasure driving since the early 1900s. Some of the most famous wended through cemeteries and beautified terrain in Buffalo, Chicago, and New York City. Congress in the 1920s made money available for the building of roads through national parks in order to make them accessible for the general public.[10]

In May of 1926, Congress passed a bill authorizing the Shenandoah National Park, a seventy-five-mile stretch of the Blue Ridge Mountains running south from Front Royal to Waynesboro. George Freeman Pollock, founder of Skyland Resort near Stonyman Mountain, is credited with selling the idea to the Department of the Interior. Pollock—not much of a businessman, but an inveterate promoter—loved the Blue Ridge Mountains, and determined at a young age to both conserve them and help others enjoy them.

The original park acreage was over 500,000, but because of unexpected costs the U.S. Department of the Interior, and Virginia, finally settled for a park of approximately 160,000 acres. This massive amount of land was acquired by the Old Dominion with the passage of a special blanket condemnation act in July of 1931 (along with follow-up condemnation orders in 1933 and 1934). This legislation allowed the state to purchase the private property it required in the counties of Albemarle, Augusta, Greene, Madison, Page, Rappahannock, Rockingham and Warren. Thousands of mountain folk were thus displaced from the farms and homes of their ancestors. Most had not been interested in selling or moving. The first years of the Great Depression slowed the development of Shenandoah National Park and the Skyline Drive.[11]

During the 1932 presidential campaign, Democratic nominee Franklin D. Roosevelt pledged "a new deal for the American people." Roosevelt took office on March 4, 1933, and immediately began tackling the massive job of revitalizing the economy. On March 21 he wrote to the 73rd Congress: "I propose to create a Civilian Conservation Corps to be used in simple work, not interfering with normal employment, and confining itself to forestry, the prevention of soil erosion, flood control, and similar projects. More important, however, than the material gains, will be the spiritual value of such work. . . . We can take a vast army of [the] unemployed out into healthful surroundings. We can eliminate to some extent the threat that enforced idleness brings to spiritual and moral stability. It is not a panacea . . . but it is an essential step in this emergency. . . ."[12] Congress responded by giving Roosevelt the go-ahead only ten days later.

The president wasted no time. Boston labor leader Robert Fechner was chosen to head the new organization; James J. McEntree from New Jersey would be his number two. A CCC Advisory Council was organized from administrators employed in the departments of Agriculture, Interior, Labor, and War. A new breed of inter-departmental cooperation had been forged. Amazingly, the first citizen enrolled in the CCC, Henry Rich of Alexandria, was inducted on April 7, 1933, only seven days after the organization's commencement—a miracle of modern government. Mr. Rich was soon thereafter sent to Camp Roosevelt just outside of Luray, Virginia.[13]

Thousands of Virginians rushed to join the CCC at its inception. In April of 1933, for example, 200 underfed youngsters applied for seventy jobs at a soon-to-be-opened camp in White Hall, Albemarle County. Times were just plain tough. Across the state's central region, scores of locally-owned businesses and factories had closed, and wanderers overfilled the lock-ups and public restrooms. Not surprisingly, crime rates were up. John Hammond Moore wrote that Albemarle County was hit less hard by the Depression because of economic activity generated by Federal and "state expenditures on roads and [University of Virginia] buildings, and [the University's] over two thousand regular students. . . ."[14] Try explaining that, however, to the Albemarle County folks who were struggling day-to-day simply to put food on the table. In the years immediately following the crash, the citizens of central Virginia had learned to tighten their belts.

Prospective CCCers were first interviewed and asked to fill out an application. According to regulations they had to be at least eighteen, but not over twenty-five. (Evidence shows, however, that many underage boys were signed up.) They had to be American citizens, of course, out of school, unmarried, and in good physical condition. (Statistics show that many early enrollees were undernourished; the average CCC youngster, in fact, gained eleven pounds in his first four months in the organization.) "The young man who enters the CCC must not be on probation or parole," wrote Kenneth Holland for the American Youth Commission, "and he must never have been convicted of an offense carrying a prison sentence of more than one year. He must be willing to stay in his camp for at least six months."[15]

One other requirement was vital. The organization preferred recruiting young men who were willing to allot to their families most of their monthly earnings; twenty-five out of thirty dollars. In this era of dire need, of course, this stipulation didn't prove to be a problem. Over 60 percent of those enrolled, in fact, cited the desire to help their families as their chief motivation. Eugene Pinney of Richmond was no exception. "Well, I couldn't find a job for several years . . . and I had nothing to do," he explained. "I had been working at ten cents an hour for ten hours, but that dried up and Daddy really needed the money. He got twenty-five dollars a month and I got five . . . that was all right by me."[16] Born in Chesterfield County in March 1913, Pinney joined the CCC in May of 1933 and was shipped up to the camp at Big Meadows, smack dab in the middle of the Skyline Drive.

Pinney's experience was echoed by Lawrence D. McDaniel of Wolftown in Madison County. Born in March 1916, McDaniel joined the CCC in 1934. "Well, I was pretty hard up back then," he remembered. "There were six of us and we needed the money . . . Yes sir, my mother needed the money."[17]

Merrill Moss of Luray had similar reasons. Born in Berkeley Springs, West Virginia, in 1919, Moss went into the CCC in 1938. His work camp was located just off the Skyline Drive. Moss's father had been disabled in a mining accident, so by the time Merrill turned eighteen the family of seven kids was ridiculously hard-pressed. "Yes, my family needed the money," he recalled, "and at first I was really ashamed . . . but then I realized we were the same as a bunch of soldiers, we had army officers and army doctors and things like that." Moss remembered another youngster from a large family who joined up to help out at home. "With his pay the family got along just fine," he said. "You know they were so poor they'd never seen a ten dollar bill. Those parents really needed that money."[18]

The nation's first CCC work camp was established April 3, 1933, at Camp Roosevelt outside of Luray, Virginia, only five miles west of Shenandoah National Park in the Page Valley. The second was Camp Dern near Skyland on the Skyline Drive. Interestingly enough, Merrill Moss began his service at Roosevelt, then was transferred to Dern up on the mountain. He remembers arriving on a truck in the dead of night. The third CCC encampment was Camp Fechner, just south of Dern at Big Meadows.[19]

When the CCC boys first arrived in the Shenandoah National Park in May of 1933, work on the Skyline Drive was well underway. Construction of the mountaintop drive had begun two years earlier during the Herbert Hoover administration. The original funding came from that year's Emergency Construction Act. By the early 1930s "the drive was envisioned as an important link in an eastern network of park-to-park highways that extended from the nation's capital to Mammoth Cave in Kentucky," wrote Park Service Historian Linda Flint McClelland.[20] Soon after his inauguration, President Roosevelt found that its closeness to Washington made it an ideal place to show off his "New Deal" brand of social legislation.

The building of the Skyline Drive was a huge cooperative effort. National Park Service landscape architects chose the path; engineers from the Bureau of Public Roads—and their many contractors— designed and built it. The lodges, cabins, and wayside stations were designed by Marcellus Wright Jr., a Richmond architect. But the park's ten camps of CCC boys provided the raw muscle that quickly advanced the work of landscaping, trail-building, ancillary construction, and overall beautification. (Six camps were set up within the park, but an additional four that were nearby also provided labor.) Between May 1933 and March 1942, more than 6,500 CCCers toiled within the boundaries of Shenandoah National Park. At any one time over 1,000 could be found along the mountaintops. They planted trees and shrubs, and graded and sloped the roadsides. They built overlooks and constructed the familiar solid stone guardrails. The youngsters also constructed fire roads and towers, log comfort stations, and picnic grounds.[21]

"Until the park was established officially on December 26, 1935," wrote Shenandoah National Park's Reed Engle, "the bulk of CCC activity took place on the narrow 100-foot right-of-way of the

Skyline Drive, in the few areas of purchased or donated land transferred to the Federal Government by the Commonwealth of Virginia, or on leased lands."[22]

The CCC camps in the Shenandoah National Park looked much like army camps. Although administration was a joint effort by the departments of Agriculture, the Interior, Labor, and War, the basic necessities—housing, sustenance, clothing, and tools—were supplied by the army. A photo taken at Camp Roosevelt in 1933, for example, shows a group of CCCers looking for all the world like army recruits sitting inside the opening of their huge U.S. Army bell tent.[23] At every CCC Camp, the rows of army tents were later replaced by permanent wooden barracks, headquarters buildings, mess halls and recreation centers. In the cold winter months, of course, staying warm and getting fed were of the upmost importance. "We slept in tents [at first], then got our barracks built," remembered Eugene Pinney, "and we had our mess hall fixed up pretty good. . . . It really got cold up there some mornings trying to get a truck started. You wore them long johns up there, yes sir, you were glad to get 'em."[24]

The initial enlistment period for the CCC was six months. CCC inductees were usually put through army conditioning but evidence indicates that most Shenandoah National Park enrollees somehow avoided this process. After six months had passed re-enlistment for another six months was possible, but the regulations placed the limit at two years. And rules, of course, are made to be broken. Joe Stollard of Stanley, Virginia, for example, worked out of the Big Meadows camp for a total of seven years. Born in Scott County, Virginia, in 1913, Stollard signed up in 1933. "A friend of mine was in town," he explained, "and this fella said 'Lets go down and join the CCC,' so we did. . . . Well, I got along just fine with the foreman up there and every time he asked if I wanted to go back in, I just said 'yes sir.'"[25]

Lawrence McDaniel stayed at Big Meadows for two years without even going through a re-enlistment process. "Nobody said nothing," he recalled, "so I stayed." Merrill Moss was warned by his foreman when his first enlistment was about up, but managed to keep his job on the mountain for another year and one-half. "You see, I wanted to stay," he related, "because that's where I met my wife."[26]

Enrollees were expected to work eight hours a day, five days a week, for $1 a day. When the family allotment was subtracted, CCCers were left with a whopping $5 a month to spend however they wished. Most of the boys went into the nearby towns on the weekends; some of them got wrapped around the infamous Virginia white lightning. "This fella named Lynch got real drunk one time," said Moss, "and when he came back he started cussing at the Chinese doctor we had. Well, he was out of there inside of a couple of days."[27]

A CCCer's daily schedule was fairly rigorous and the work was backbreaking, but most of the youngsters thrived in the outdoor environment. "We would get up at 5:30," remembered Moss, "and have our breakfast right away. Then we'd go out to the work site. Lunch was at 12:00 noon and quitting time was at 4:00." Eugene Pinney worked for a while as a cook at the Big Meadows camp. "Imagine cooking for 206 fellas, three times a day," he said. "We fixed ham and chicken and vegetables. I remember the mess sergeant figured it cost the government nine cents a meal to feed them fellas." Army recruits are famous for complaining about service food; not so with the CCCers. "That food was good, and they'd bring us lunch on the back of a truck," recalled Merrill Moss. "They even had a gallon container of jelly to dip your bread in."[28]

Of course it was just the kind of work that stimulates a healthy appetite. Joe Stollard remembered dressing down the banks along the Skyline Drive. He also laid sod and cut wood. "I can't grumble about it," he said, "'cause it was something for me to do." McDaniel said he "sloped banks and cleaned up the side of the road, kinda beautified it . . . and [he] pulled up the gooseberries." He also wielded an ax and a cross-cut saw. Merrill Moss worked on the trails. "I built trails from Skyland to Old Rag Mountain," he said. "You see, our camp had a lot of city boys who didn't know how to use an ax, but I had lots of experience cutting timber. In fact, they signed me up as a lumberjack. John Ash was our foreman, and as long as you done your work it was OK. He had the best ax in the company and I had number two."[29]

Eugene Pinney worked alongside the road, removing chunks of rock that had been blasted. "We was the front-end loaders," he explained, "because we didn't have that kind of equipment. We'd use these special rigs to lift the big ones. I've seen seven fellas trying to move just one rock." He later drove a ton-and-a-half Chevrolet Department of the Interior truck. "We brought logs and wood—lots of dead chestnuts—off the mountain and gave it to people who needed it." Merrill Moss explained how he learned to drive on the Blue Ridge trails. "I started off in small trucks then went on to bigger and bigger ones," he said. "I got lots of experience that way."[30]

And what an experience it was. To many, it was their first time away from home. "Oh yeah, it was my first time away," said Pinney, "and it taught you to get along with other people and a whole bunch of other things. We enjoyed it and had a real nice time. I met some mighty nice fellas up there." Moss's time in the CCC was much the same. "Well, it gave me experience away from home," he recalled, "and it was just like the army. It helped me grow up, and I know it helped those city boys."[31]

Many of Shenandoah National Park's CCC boys were from outside the state of Virginia. "There were people up there from everywhere," remembered Lawrence McDaniel, "and we were all just like brothers. We kinda looked after each other." Sometimes, however, there were fights. "The city boys and the country boys got along okay in our camp," related Merrill Moss, "but one time they had to move a bunch of Maryland boys out because of North and South fights." In the 1930s, of course, the Civil War was only seventy years in the past.[32]

The legacy of Shenandoah National Park's CCC work camps is truly impressive. Over one hundred miles of ridge-top roadway were landscaped and beautified with CCC labor. The boys also took part in the construction of sixty-nine scenic overlooks and six picnic grounds. They cut and improved trails, and built stone gutters and guardrails. The youngsters constructed maintenance buildings, comfort stations, and shelters. In the process the CCC pulled the boys up out of poverty and gave them a jump start into manhood.

On April 29, 1997, the Skyline Drive Historic District was listed in the National Register of Historic Places. National Park Service historian Linda Flint McClelland called the Skyline Drive "[o]ne of the most complete and extensive landscapes shaped by the CCC in the program's nine-year history."[33] And the vistas are simply phenomenal. From the drive and its overlooks today's visitor can gaze across an incredibly wondrous region of mountains, sheltered hollows, dashing streams, and forests. These views are a lasting reminder of the over 6,500 young men who labored on the mountaintops between 1933 and 1942.

All of the CCCers I spoke with were proud of their work and proud to tell their stories. I'll never forget them. As I concluded my interview with eighty-four-year-old Joe Stollard he surprised me by saying that he wasn't going to tell me good-bye. "There's no such thing as good-bye in this world," he said matter-of-factly. "Why, you and I . . . we'll just meet again somewhere else." I can only hope that place is half as beautiful as the Skyline Drive he helped create.[34]

Endnotes

1. One of the most popular Depression-era songs, "Beans, Bacon, and Gravy" was claimed by at least three songwriters. It was recorded by Pete Seeger in the 1950s.

2. My apologies to Charles Dickens.

3. Galbraith, John Kenneth, *The Great Crash: 1929* (Boston, 1955), pg. 2.

4. Meltzer, Milton, *Brother, Can You Spare a Dime?* (New York, 1969), pg. 42.

5. Ibid., pg. 49.

6. Rodgers, Cleveland, *The Roosevelt Program* (New York, 1933), pgs. 117-25.

7. Myers, Andrew H., "The Creation of the Shenandoah National Park: Albemarle County Cultures in Conflict," *The Magazine of Albemarle County History* (Charlottesville, 1993), Vol. 51, pg. 68.

8. Lambert, Darwin, *The Undying Past of Shenandoah National Park* (Boulder, Colo., 1989), pg. 200. For more information about the intense competition between states, see: Whisnant, Anne Mitchell, "Routing The Parkway, 1934," at http://docsouth.unc.edu/blueridgeparkway/overlooks/competing_routes/

9. Myers, "The Creation of the Shenandoah National Park," pg. 68.

10. Belles, Christopher, "They Built a Road in the Sky," Charlottesville *Daily Progress*, March 1, 1997.

11. Myers, "The Creation of the Shenandoah National Park," pgs. 80-1.

12. Quoted in: Huddleston, Connie, *Georgia's Civilian Conservation Corps* (Charleston, SC, 2009), pg. 8.

13. Unattributed, "Shenandoah," *Country Living Magazine* (Harlan, IA, 1983), Vol. 5, No. 3, pgs. 19-20.

14. Moore, John Hammond, *Albemarle; Jefferson's Country, 1727-1976* (Charlottesville, 1976), pgs. 385-86.

15. Holland, Kenneth, *Youth in the CCC* (Washington D.C., 1942), pg. 48.

16. Eugene Pinney telephone interview conducted November 21, 1998.

17. Lawrence D. McDaniel telephone interview conducted November 22, 1998.

18. Merrill Moss telephone interview conducted November 22, 1998.

19. "Civilian Conservation Corps Quick Reference Fact Sheet" published by Shenandoah National Park (1997), pg. 2, and Merrill Moss interview.

20. McClelland, Linda Flint, "Skyline Drive Historic District; A Meeting Place of Culture and Nature," *CRM: The Journal of Heritage Stewardship* (Washington, D.C., 1998), No. 1, pg. 13.

21. Ibid., pg. 14.

22. Engle, Reed L., "Shenandoah; Not Without the CCC," *CRM: The Journal of Heritage Stewardship* (Washington, D.C., 1998), No. 1, pg. 22.

23. For a wonderful selection of Skyline Drive CCC camp photos, see: Cohen, Stan, *The Tree Army: A Pictorial History of the Civilian Conservation Corps, 1933-1942* (Missoula, MO, 1980).

24. Pinney interview.

25. Joe Stollard telephone interview conducted November 25, 1998.

26. McDaniel and Moss interviews.

27. Moss interview.

28. Pinney and Moss interviews.

29. Stollard and McDaniel interviews.

30. Pinney and Moss interviews.

31. Pinney and Moss interviews.

32. McDaniel and Moss interviews.

33. McClelland, "Skyline Drive Historic District," pg. 13.

34. Stollard interview.

Tech. Sgt. Frank Dabney Peregoy (1916 – 1944).
(Photo by U.S. Army.)

"Best Enemy-Fighter in the World": The Frank Dabney Peregoy Story

War is three things. It is a way of deciding great differences among people. That is the politicians' war. It is a game of infinite complexity. That is the generals' war. And it is a personal experience of weariness, hatred, terror, filth, and occasional heroism and humor. That is the soldiers' war.[1]
– War correspondent Charles C. Wertenbaker of Charlottesville, 1944

The Normandy town of Grandcamp-les-Bains lies ten miles west of Omaha Beach on the main coastal highway. Prior to World War II, the 1,500 inhabitants had occupied themselves primarily with bringing in the day's catch, and catering to those who had come to enjoy the pleasant beaches. On the afternoon of June 8, 1944, however, the quaint fishing village was anything but tranquil. As American troops approached from the east, German forces in the town opened-up with heavy mortar and machine-gun fire. Their positions seemed impregnable. On D-Day plus two, Grandcamp-les-Bains certainly looked like it was going to be a tough nut.

"The town was on a knoll," remembered Carl D. "Chubby" Proffitt of Charlottesville, Virginia, a veteran of Company K of the 116th Infantry. "The ground dipped down from there. . . . I remember in particular a huge church steeple. . . . The Germans were dug-in in front of the town, and had fortifications all around it."[2] In order to deny access they had mined the highway. Adding to the man-made defenses was a marshy stream flowing north toward the sea which the Germans had purposely flooded, making it a virtual moat.

115

In order to assail Grandcamp the Americans had to traverse the bog over a small bridge; and attack uphill across an open, 200-yard-long field. Scattered patches of high grass would afford the only means of cover. "It was the only way in," said Proffitt. Earlier in the day Grandcamp had been hammered by huge naval shells lobbed-in by the British cruiser *Glasgow*. Unfortunately, this one-hour bombardment had failed to dislodge, or even discourage, the German defenders.[3]

The first assault of the afternoon was made by men of the 5th Ranger Battalion. Behind them was deployed a 29th Division unit—the 3rd Battalion, 116th Infantry—Virginia boys from Charlottesville and the central Virginia Piedmont. Crouching low, the Rangers crossed the bridge and fanned out. On the enemy side the highway was blocked by a Sherman tank minus one of its treads. It had struck a mine. Picking their way up the slope, the Rangers were greeted by a vicious hail of metal. Machine-gun rounds kicked up the earth at their feet. Mortar shells split the air with ear-deafening blasts. The Rangers dropped and attempted to return the fire. Many of them never rose again. With their advance stopped cold they sent back for help. Now it was the 116th's turn.[4]

Evening was fast approaching as a portion of the 3rd Battalion, 116th Infantry—perhaps as many as 250 men—began its advance. Beyond the marsh "K and L Companies moved through the Rangers," wrote Joseph H. Ewing in his history of the 29th Division, and attacked right up the road. "We went right through them," echoed "Chubby" Proffitt of K Company, "and continued right against Grandcamp. . . . [The Rangers] had already taken heavy casualties, you see, in the landing" [two days earlier].[5]

Company K hit the Germans on the right of the line, along the highway and to the north. They immediately encountered stiff resistance. Proffitt remembered the Germans opening-up as soon as the Virginians came into view. "They pinned us down real sharply," he said. "Repeated assaults," wrote Gertrude Dana Parlier, "were turned back by machine-gun and rifle fire." Company K's commander—Captain William G. Pingley, Jr. of Winchester, Virginia—was killed leading his men forward. It was obvious to many on that bullet-swept slope that something else, something different, had to be done.[6]

A battalion officer later recalled seeing one man from Company K—one American G.I.—crouching forward through the withering fire that commanded that hillside. He was slowly working his way to the crest, armed only with his rifle, bayonet, and a few hand grenades. It seemed miraculous that he wasn't being hit. Taking the situation into his own hands, Technical Sergeant Frank Peregoy of Charlottesville, Virginia, . . . was going-it . . . alone.[7]

Frank Dabney Peregoy was born on April 10, 1916, in the town of Faber, Nelson County, Virginia. His parents were Suzie Edward Allen and James Eligh Peregoy, a farmer and itinerant laborer. "Between the years of 1922-23," wrote relative Janet L. Perriello, "James and Suzie moved their family to Esmont in Albemarle County. They made their home across the road from James's brother, John Dabney."[8]

According to Perriello, "Frank was the second born of eleven children and was the oldest son." The youngest of the family, Don Peregoy, maintained that only eight of the children reached maturity, four boys and four girls. Several had been stillborn. Mother Suzie, unfortunately, died in 1931 and James followed her to the grave but four years later. "Orphaned at age nineteen," wrote Perriello, "Frank kept the family together for a short while, but then they separated to live with other family members."[9]

Frank Dabney Peregoy, therefore, came of age during the country's worst economic period—the Great Depression—while his family was dissolving all around him. In response he became very protective. "We had a great big grapevine swing out near the house and we were all up there, you know, swinging," remembered brother Don Peregoy, ten years Frank's junior.

"Some boys from somewhere else were there, about Frank's size, see," he said, "and one of them was pushing me. I said I wanted to quit, see, but he said 'Oh, no, you can go again' and he pushed me . . . so I let go of the swing. . . . I can remember it so clearly. I dropped down into the leaves and dirt; it didn't hurt me one bit. But Frank runs to me and says he was giving the others hell for swinging me again . . . and they left. Frank was ready to tangle with them over me, see."

On another occasion a local man was harassing one of Frank's little sisters. "She was just a young girl, nine or ten," recalled Don. "Some man would come out in the morning when she was going to school and say 'my, what a pretty little girl you are'. . . . Well, it frightened her because he was doing it persistently—so she told Frank. So, Frank sneaked along behind her, you know, going to school. And the man did come out and was talking to her . . . so Frank stepped out and told the man that he wanted him to leave her alone. The man apologized . . . and never bothered her again."

"The important thing, I would think, from a historical viewpoint, would be not to elevate this family," said Don Peregoy. "We were dirt poor, mountaineers. . . . My older sister didn't finish school. Frank, as far as I know, never graduated from high school. They went to a very small school, the ones in the family that did go, called Old Dominion School."[10]

With the death of his mother, Frank Peregoy was forced to quit pursuing an education and go to work on the farm full-time. The younger kids really needed him. "He had learned how to work hard real early in his life," sister Daisy McReady told the *Daily Progress*. "Those were hard years, but we lived on our garden crops, and we raised bees so we had honey. We'd sell the honey for fifteen cents a pint and berries we'd pick for ten cents a gallon."[11]

James Peregoy's death in 1935, as mentioned above, caused the further breakup of the family. Daisy, for example, went to live with an older couple near Scottsville. Nineteen-year-old Frank Peregoy moved in with William and Florence Sampson in Charlottesville. Across the street was a lumber yard. "Uncle Ed Hildebrand was a yard foreman at Barnes Lumber Co.," remembered Don, "and when Frank left Green Mountain in Esmont he went to work for him. . . . My uncle didn't want to hire him at first because he said Frank was too small. . . . Later he said Frank was one of the best workers he had. And that was a fairly rough job, you know, throwing that lumber around."[12]

Don Peregoy was quick to emphasize that, growing up, "he didn't see a great deal" of big brother Frank. But what he did see impressed him. "He stacked up then with the other guys working there [at Barnes Lumber], maybe just a shade shorter, you know, but physically he was quite sure of himself. . . . Some mention was made then of what big hands he had, you know, big fists. An uncle of mine used to say he wanted to get Frank into boxing, saying he would promote him. . . . I heard people in the family talking one time that Frank was in jail for being in a fight."

Whether the story about being in trouble is true or not, Frank Peregoy was a popular young man. He was quiet and unassuming. "He was my brother," said Don, "and I could stand by his side, see, and listen to him talk to someone else. I liked him because he was my brother. Everyone seemed to like him."[13]

Roy Sampson, William and Florence's son, told the *Daily Progress* what it was like living with Frank Peregoy during approximately the same period. "I was just a kid when [he] first came to live with us," he recounted. "He would take us kids and give us wooden sticks for rifles and tell us we were fighting a war. . . . He'd tease you all day if you let him. Yes sir, Frank was a good boy."[14]

It should, perhaps, come as no surprise that the strapping youngster was interested in "playing" war, for by 1935, Frank Peregoy had been a member of the National Guard for four years. "According to military records," wrote Perriello, "Frank enlisted in the Monticello Guard on July 5, 1931. At the time, he was only fifteen years old. Military records, however, indicate that Frank was sixteen years old, with the record indicating a birthdate of April 10, 1915...." Either the military made an error, or Peregoy had lied about his age. Little brother Don smiled when he heard of this confusion. "You have to understand," he explained, "that during the Depression a lot of fibbin' was going-on about people's ages. Young boys needed jobs to help support their families." Frank had simply told a white lie to get in.[15]

And then there's the matter of the correct spelling of the family name. Military records show it spelled P-e-r-e-g-o-r-y, adding an extra "r." The state historical marker at Emmett Street and University Avenue also spells it that way. Both, unfortunately, are wrong. "All the family spells it P-e-r-e-g-o-y," said Don. "Frank spelled it that way too.... Now I will assume this: that some official or clerk wrote down P-e-r-e-g-o-r-y ... and Frank, he didn't give a damn. I don't think it mattered to him.... I have been told it's French. And I have been told that great-great-great-grandpa came here [to central Virginia] to work in the orchards."[16]

Frank Peregoy was officially inducted into federal service—for a year's training—on February 3, 1941. He had already grown accustomed to hard work and hard living: military life suited him. Peregoy thrived on the regular exercise and food, and the hearty army camaraderie. John Taylor of Albemarle County recalled for the *Daily Progress* how, during bayonet practice against targets and dummies, Peregoy "went through the course [and] just tore it all to pieces. I mean, he was sticking and smashing the stuffing out of those dummies like you would not believe."[17]

When the Monticello Guard returned to Charlottesville five months later—to take part in the Fourth of July festivities—Frank stayed around for the weekend. On Saturday, July 5, he married Bessie Geneva Kirby, one of the waitresses at Kirby's beer joint on Monticello Road south of Charlottesville. He would later joke with his army pals that, unhappily, he had spent more nights with his rifle, than he had with his bride.[18]

In active service Charlottesville's Monticello Guard became Company K of the 3rd Battalion, 116th Infantry Regiment—one of three regiments, along with artillery and support companies, in the U.S. Army's 29th Division. This particular National Guard force was known as the Blue-and-Gray Division because it incorporated units from Pennsylvania, Maryland, Virginia, and the District of Columbia: northerners and southerners. The 29th's well-trained National Guardsmen wore the distinctive ying-and-yang-symboled patch in blue and gray.[19]

Like the division's other units, the 116th Infantry bore a proud lineage. It was descended from the 2nd Virginia Regiment—a militia unit first formed in 1760—and had been led by Col. George Washington in the French and Indian War and Patrick Henry in the early days of the American Revolution. At First Manassas, in the Civil War, the men of the 2nd Virginia had "stood like a stonewall" with Confederate Gen. Thomas Jonathan Jackson.[20] In the world-shattering struggle that was fast approaching the brave soldiers of the 116th, and the 29th Division, would be called upon to stand up against a more numerous, and more hideous, foe.

On Sunday, January 11, 1942—thirty-five days after Pearl Harbor—Frank Peregoy became the 29th Division's first war-time hero. Early that frost-bitten morning elements of the 116th Infantry were patrolling the North Carolina coast, close to New Berne, when a Company K weapons' carrier slid on an icy road and nose-dived into the deep waters of an adjacent canal. Most of the men swam out but a quick roll-call revealed that Priv. Stanley P. Major was missing and obviously still underwater. (Evidently, a strap from his backpack was caught on the truck.)

Without a thought, without hesitation, Peregoy dove back into the frigid water—an army knife clutched between his teeth Tarzanstyle. Slicing his way through the vehicle's tarpaulin cover Frank swam down into the back of the truck and cut the unfortunate private loose. When he pushed the seemingly lifeless body back up through the hole other men from Company K grabbed it and pulled it ashore. Thankfully, although Major had lost consciousness, he was revived several hours later, back in camp.

For his unselfish act of bravery Corp. Frank Peregoy was decorated with the Soldier's Medal, America's highest non-combat award. In the special ceremony—held at Fort A. P. Hill near Fredericksburg, Virginia, on June 17, 1942—Peregoy stood on the podium alongside Maj. Gen. Leonard T. Gerow, the division commander. When members of the 116th Regimental Combat Team formally marched past in review—eyes right!—Peregoy shyly returned their salute. As soon as he had been pinned with the red, white, and blue ribbon, the modest hero, embarrassed by all the hoopla, quietly returned to his daily routine.[21]

The 116th Infantry was shipped off to England, aboard the *Queen Mary*, in September of 1942. Assigned to Tidworth Barracks, near Andover, much of the next twenty months was spent in intensive training. The guardsmen were marched all over the beautiful English countryside under the deadweight of their backpacks—marched until a twenty-five-mile day became routine. They also practiced amphibious landings.[22]

Peregoy, in the process, learned everything about his rifle, inside and out. After the war a 3rd Battalion officer commented to Charlottesville-native Frank Hartman—himself a World War II veteran—that Peregoy, when it came to taking apart and reassembling his weapon, "was gifted . . . he could do it blindfolded."[23] In England, Frank Peregoy also became a deadly marksman.

On the morning of June 6, 1944, Tech. Sgt. Frank Peregoy was riding the choppy waters of the English Channel just offshore of the Normandy beach code-named "Omaha." The 29th Division had been assigned this sector for the massive Allied D-Day invasion: the 116th Infantry was to lead the division ashore. The division's first wave landed at approximately 6:30 a.m. The second wave—the wave that included Peregoy's 3rd Battalion—starting hitting the beach about an hour later.

As the landing craft's doors splashed open, the Virginians vividly remembered their chaplain's quote from Isaiah 43: "When you pass through the waters I will be with you . . . and when you walk through the fire you will not be burned."[24]

"Luckily our boat-team section didn't take any casualties coming in," recalled "Chubby" Proffitt of Company K, "but our regiment lost over 800." Through a veritable hailstorm of German gunfire the 1st and 3rd Battalions of the 116th—along with the attached 5th Ranger Battalion—fought their way to the crest of the bluffs overlooking the beach. They became the first elements of the 29th Division to pierce the enemy's first line of defense.[25]

From the top of the rise the men of Company K, 3rd Battalion, could gaze back down into a hellhole. "It looked like a great junk yard," wrote Charlottesville-born Wertenbaker, including "landing craft impaled on obstacles, blown by mines, [and] shattered by shellfire. . . . [T]here was a bulldozer with its guts spattered over the sand and another with its occupants so spattered, an arm here, a leg there, a piece of pulp over yonder. There were discarded things all over the beach: lifebelts, cartridge clips, canteens, pistol belts, bayonets, K-rations." Among these inanimate objects were the human remains of the 116th Infantry—hundreds of their dead and dying.[26]

Two days later, on the afternoon of June 8, the Virginians of Company K, 3rd Battalion, found themselves facing a very obstinate

German force dug-in at Grandcamp-les-Bains. After the Monticello Guard had been under fire for two hours Frank Peregoy made his move. Half running, half crouching the plucky technical sergeant quickly advanced on the first German trench line. From close range he opened up with unerring aim. Pow, pow, pow rang the shots from Peregoy's M-1. "When his clip would fly out, he'd stick another in it," Company K veteran John Taylor later told the *Daily Progress*. "After he had gone quite a ways he starts pulling out hand grenades and throwing them around. I don't know where he got them all from."[27]

At the military crest—at the foe's first line—Frank Peregoy attached his bayonet and gamely jumped in. Obviously he wasn't concerned with the odds. In the ditch Peregoy "found himself among a squad of enemy riflemen and immediately engaged them," wrote an officer who witnessed the struggle. Faster than they were able to react to his sudden appearance Peregoy shot and killed eight German soldiers. Three more surrendered. Then, with his prisoners in tow, the one-man platoon advanced on the enemy's main position using the trench for cover.[28]

This next objective was a deeply dug-in machine-gun nest. As Peregoy approached the weapon's staccato fire—a regular, rat-tat-tat-tat—was still pinning-down his company mates. Frank took it on with hand grenades. With a few ground-shaking explosions—from grenades well-tossed by the Virginian—Peregoy "destroyed the position," wrote the battalion officer, "and forced the surrender of thirty-two other German riflemen." In all these heroics Frank hadn't received so much as a scratch.[29]

Peregoy's amazing feat had an immediate effect on the battlefield. "The fact is, the men who were watching all this were so inspired," recalled C. B. Smith, "that they charged toward the Germans." At this the enemy troops that still remained in the pillboxes routed to the rear. Grandcamp fell.[30]

Told a few weeks later of his brother's astounding accomplishments Don Peregoy was not surprised. "He was my big brother, see, and even though I didn't see him very often he still maintained that big brother persona in my imagination . . . and he could do anything that he wanted to do, anything. . . . So if it came to fightin' the enemy, he was the best enemy-fighter in the world."[31]

Unfortunately, a boy's imagination and cold reality are often at odds. "Best enemy-fighter" Frank Dabney Peregoy was killed in action on June 14, 1944, only six days after the combat at Grandcamp.

"I was within thirty feet of him when it happened," recalled Company K's "Chubby" Proffitt, "just across the hedgerow. He was leading men through a gap . . . attacking across a field. The Germans waited until he got into the opening, then they let him have it. . . . I crawled to where he was and he was already dead."[32]

Peregoy was posthumously awarded the Medal of Honor in a ceremony at the Charlottesville City Armory on June 4, 1945. In attendance were close friends, relatives, units of the Virginia State Guard, and returned members of the Monticello Guard, Company K, 116th Infantry. Brig. Gen. E. R. Warner McCabe presented the nation's highest award to Bessie Kirby Peregoy, Frank's widow. "You will have the comfort and consolation and satisfaction of knowing," he told her, "that your heroic husband's memory will live forever in the hearts of his country and his valiant deeds will live in the hearts of his fellow citizens."[33]

Today, Frank Dabney Peregoy rests near the beaches of Normandy, beneath a white stone marker in the U.S. cemetery at St. Laurent-Sur-Mer. Thousands of other American headstones surround him.

Endnotes

1. Wertenbacker, Charles C., *Invasion!* (New York, 1944), pg. 1.

2. Interview with former Tech. Sgt. Carl D. "Chubby" Proffitt on 9/15/99. At the time of the 1999 interview he was eighty years old.

3. Proffitt interview; Ewing, Joseph H., *29 Let's Go!; A History of the 29th Infantry Division in World War* II (Washington, D.C., 1948), pg. 64.

4. Parlier, Gertrude Dana, *Pursuits of War; The People of Charlottesville and Albemarle County, Virginia, in the Second World War* (Charlottesville, 1948), pg. 236.

5. Proffitt interview; Ewing, *29 Let's Go!*, pg. 64.

6. Proffitt interview; Parlier, *Pursuits of War*, pg. 236.

7. Charlottesville *Daily Progress*, May 29, 1945.

8. Perriello, Janet L., "For the Record; A Short Biography of Frank Dabney Peregory (Peregoy)" (unpublished, updated 2011). Perriello is a second cousin to Frank D. Peregoy.

9. Perriello, "For the Record"; interview with Don Peregoy, Frank's youngest brother, 9/19/99. Born in Esmont in 1926, at the time of the interview Don was seventy-two years old.

10. Ibid.

11. Maurer, David, "Soldier learned to care for others at a young age," Charlottesville *Daily Progress*, May 29, 1994.

12. Don Peregoy interview.

13. Ibid.

14. Maurer, Charlottesville *Daily Progress*, May 29, 1994.

15. Perriello, "For the Record"; Don Peregoy interview.

16. Ibid.

17. Charlottesville *Daily Progress*, May 29, 1945.

18. Perriello, "For the Record."

19. Ewing, *29 Let's Go!*, pgs. xi-xii. According to Ewing: "The 29th Infantry Division's shoulder insignia of blue and gray, adapted from the design of the *monad*, the Korean symbol of life, shows blue and gray colors forming one into the other, to represent the reintegration of North and South into a harmonious unity."

20. Ibid, pg. xii.

21. Unattributed, "Technical Sergeant Frank D. Peregory; United States Army and Monticello Guards" (unpublished), Albemarle Charlottesville Historical Society files; Perriello, "For the Record."

22. Ewing, *29 Let's Go!*, pgs. 13-18.

23. Frank Hartman interview, 9/25/99.

24. Proffitt interview.

25. Ibid.

26. Wertenbaker, *Invasion!*, pgs. 53-54.

27. Charlottesville *Daily Progress*, May 29, 1945; also quoted in Maurer, David, "Local hero didn't even know he'd won nation's highest honor," Charlottesville *Daily Progress*, June 5, 1994.

28. Ibid.

29. Ibid.

30. Maurer, Charlottesville *Daily Progress*, June 5, 1994.

31. Don Peregoy interview.

32. Proffitt interview.

33. Unattributed, "Technical Sergeant Frank D. Peregory."

SELECT BIBLIOGRAPHY

MANUSCRIPTS

Liebwan, Rosanna, & McQuaid, Matilda, "The Rise of the Black Baptist Church; A Study of Ten Black Baptist Churches in Albemarle County" (unpublished, Albemarle Charlottesville Historical Society, 1983).

Perriello, Janet L., "For the Record; A Short Biography of Frank Dabney Peregory (Peregoy)" (unpublished, updated 2011).

Unattributed, "Civilian Conservation Corps Quick Reference Fact Sheet" (Shenandoah National Park, 1997).

Unattributed, "Technical Sergeant Frank D. Peregory; United States Army and Monticello Guards" (unpublished, Albemarle Charlottesville Historical Society).

ARTICLES

Dabney, Virginius, "Jack Jouett's Ride," *American Heritage Magazine* (December, 1961), Vol. 13, Issue 1.

Engle, Reed L., "Shenandoah; Not Without the CCC," *CRM: The Journal of Heritage Stewardship* (Washington, D.C., 1998), No. 1.

Harrison, James Albert, "New Glimpses of Poe (II)," *The Independent* (New York, Sept. 13, 1900), Vol. LII, No. 2702.

Hauck, Louise Platt "The Pony Express Celebration," *Missouri Historical Review* (Columbia, Missouri). Vol. XVII.

Kent, Charles W., "Poe's Student Days at the University of Virginia," *The Bookman Illustrated Magazine of Literature and Life* (New York, July 1901), Vol. 13.

Maurer, David A., "Pony Express Pioneer Left His Mark on VMI," *VMI Alumni Review* (Lexington, 1993), Vol. 69, No. 4.

McClelland, Linda Flint, "Skyline Drive Historic District; A Meeting Place of Culture and Nature," *CRM: The Journal of Heritage Stewardship* (Washington, D.C., 1998), No. 1.

Myers, Andrew H., "The Creation of the Shenandoah National Park: Albemarle County Cultures in Conflict," *The Magazine of Albemarle County History* (Charlottesville, 1993), Vol. 51.

Nichols, Frederick Doveton, "A Day to Remember; The Burning of the Rotunda, 1895," *The Magazine of Albemarle County History* (Charlottesville, 1959), Vol. XVII.

Poe, Edgar A., "A Tale of the Ragged Mountains," *Complete Tales & Poems of Edgar Allan Poe* (New York, 1938).

128

Poe, Edgar A., "The Literati of New York City.—No. IV; Some Honest Opinions at Random Respecting Their Autorial Merits, With Occasional Words of Personality," *Godey's Lady's Book* (New York, August 1846).

Poe, Edgar A., "William Wilson," *Complete Tales & Poems of Edgar Allan Poe* (New York, 1938).

Read, B. M., "Ben Ficklin 1849 and the Pony Express," *VMI Alumni Review* (Lexington, summer 1973).

Schulman, Gayle M., "Learning in the Charlottesville Freedman's School: the First Jefferson School," *The Magazine of Albemarle County History* (Charlottesville, 2007), Vol. 64.

Stovall, Floyd, "Edgar Poe and the University of Virginia," *The Virginia Quarterly Review* (Charlottesville, Spring 1967), Vol. 43, No. 2.

Tapp, Hambleton, "Jouett's Desperate Ride, The Lost Chapter of the American Revolution: Jack Jouett, Virginian, Kentuckian, *University of Kentucky Magazine* (Lexington, ____).

Unattributed, "Shenandoah," *Country Living Magazine* (Harlan, IA, 1983), Vol. 5, No. 3.

NEWSPAPERS

Belles, Christopher, "They Built a Road in the Sky," Charlottesville *Daily Progress*, March 1, 1997.

Charlottesville *Chronicle*, March 17, 1871.

Charlottesville *Daily Progress*, January 17, 1987.

Charlottesville *Daily Progress*, May 29, 1945.

Maurer, David, "Soldier learned to care for others at a young age," Charlottesville *Daily Progress*, May 29, 1994.

Maurer, David, Charlottesville *Daily Progress*, June 5, 1994.

Unattributed, "Mount Zion Baptist Church; A Century of Christian Service," Charlottesville *Daily Progress*, January 7, 1967.

Unattributed, "Ben Ficklin Now Credited With Pony Express Origin," San Angelo, Texas, *Evening Standard*, April 29, 1948.

Via, Vera V., "Looking Back," Charlottesville *Daily Progress*, March 24, 1955.

SECONDARY SOURCES

Anthony, Katharine, *Dolly Madison; Her Life and Times* (Garden City, N.Y., 1949).

Austerman, Wayne R., *Sharps Rifles and Spanish Mules; The San Antonio-El Paso Mail, 1851-1881* (College Station, Texas, 1985).

Britton, Rick, *Jefferson; A Monticello Sampler* (Buena Vista, Virginia, 2008).

Bruce, Philip Alexander, *History of the University of Virginia, 1819-1919; The Lengthened Shadow of One Man* (New York, 1921), Vol. IV.

Cauthen, Irby B. Jr., *Edgar Allan Poe at the University* (Charlottesville, 1999).

Chapman, Arthur, *The Pony Express; The Record of a Romantic Adventure in Business* (New York, 1932).

Clark, Allen Culling, ed., *Life & Letters of Dolly Madison* (Washington, D.C., 1914).

Cohen, Stan, *The Tree Army: A Pictorial History of the Civilian Conservation Corps, 1933-1942* (Missoula, MO, 1980).

Collins, Lewis, *Historical Sketches of Kentucky* (Mercer County, Kentucky, 1968).

Dabney, Virginius, *Mr. Jefferson's University* (Charlottesville, 1981).

Dean, Elizabeth Lippincott, *Dolly Madison; The Nation's Hostess* (Boston, 1928).

Ewing, Joseph H., *29 Let's Go!; A History of the 29th Infantry Division in World War II* (Washington, D.C., 1948).

Faragher, John Mack, ed., *My Father, Daniel Boone: the Draper Interviews with Nathan Boone* (New York, 1992).

Hafen, Le Roy R., *The Overland Mail, 1849-1869; Promoter of Settlement, Precursor of Railroads* (Cleveland, 1926).

Galbraith, John Kenneth, *The Great Crash: 1929* (Boston, 1955).

Goodwin, Maud Wilder, *Women of Colonial and Revolutionary Times; Dolly Madison* (New York, 1911).

Griswold, Rufus Wilmot, "Memoir of the Author," *The Works of the Late Edgar Allan Poe* (New York, 1850-56), Vol. 3.

Hogan, Pendleton, *The Lawn; A Guide to Jefferson's University* (Charlottesville, 1987).

Holland, Kenneth, *Youth in the CCC* (Washington D.C., 1942).

Huddleston, Connie, *Georgia's Civilian Conservation Corps* (Charleston, SC, 2009).

Hunt, Gaillard, ed., and Smith, Margaret Bayard, *The First Forty Years of Washington Society: Portrayed By the Family Letters of Mrs. Samuel Harrison Smith* (New York, 1906).

Hunt-Jones, Conover, *Dolley and the "Great Little Madison"* (Washington, D.C., 1977).

Lambert, Darwin, *The Undying Past of Shenandoah National Park* (Boulder, Colorado, 1989).

Lay, K. Edward, *The Architecture of Jefferson Country; Charlottesville and Albemarle County, Virginia* (Charlottesville, 2000).

Malone, Dumas, *Jefferson and His Time; The Sage of Monticello* (Boston, 1981).

Meltzer, Milton, *Brother, Can You Spare a Dime?* (New York, 1969).

McAllister, J. T., *Virginia Militia in the Revolutionary War* (Hot Springs, Virginia, 1913).

McKinney, Richard I., *Keeping the Faith; A History of The First Baptist Church, 1863-1980, In Light of Its Times* (Charlottesville, 1981).

Montgomery, William E., *Under Their Own Vine and Fig Tree; The African-American Church in the South, 1865-1900* (Baton Rouge, 1993).

Moore, John Hammond, *Albemarle; Jefferson's Country, 1727-1976* (Charlottesville, 1976).

Parlier, Gertrude Dana, *Pursuits of War; The People of Charlottesville and Albemarle County, Virginia, in the Second World War* (Charlottesville, 1948).

Patton, John S., and Doswell, Sallie J., *The University of Virginia; Glimpses of Its Past and Present* (Lynchburg, 1900).

Peterson, Merrill D., ed., *James Madison; A Biography in His Own Words* (New York, 1974), Vol. 2.

Quinn, Arthur Hobson, *Edgar Allan Poe: A Critical Biography* (New York, 1941).

Randall, Henry S., *The Life of Thomas Jefferson* (New York, 1858).

Rawlings, Mary, ed., *Early Charlottesville; Recollections of James Alexander, 1828-1874* (Charlottesville, 1942).

Robinson, Morgan Poitiaux, *The Burning of the Rotunda; Being a Sketch of the Partial Destruction of the University of Virginia (1895)* (Richmond, 1905).

Rodgers, Cleveland, *The Roosevelt Program* (New York, 1933).

Selby, John E., *The Revolution in Virginia, 1775-1783* (Williamsburg, 1988).

Stanton, Lucia, *Free Some Day; The African-American Families of Monticello* (Charlottesville, 2000).

Tarleton, Banastre, *A History of the Campaigns of 1780 and 1781* (London, 1787).

Taylor, A. A., *The Negro in the Reconstruction of Virginia* (New York, 1969).

Tucker, George, *Life of Thomas Jefferson* (Philadelphia, 1837), Vol. II.

Twain, Mark, *Roughing It* (Hartford, 1872).

Vandiver, Frank E., *Ploughshares Into Swords; Josiah Gorgas and Confederate Ordnance* (Austin, 1952).

Vaughan, Joseph Lee, and Gianniny, Omer Allan, Jr., *Thomas Jefferson's Rotunda Restored, 1973-76; A Pictorial Review With Commentary* (Charlottesville, 1981).

Wertenbacker, Charles C., *Invasion!* (New York, 1944).

Wills, Garry, *Mr. Jefferson's University* (Washington, D.C., 2002).

Woods, Edgar, *Albemarle County in Virginia* (Charlottesville, 1901).

INDEX

Page numbers in italics refer to images.

University of Virginia (U.Va.), 41, 57, 60, 64, 105; Annex, 92, 96; Bronze bell, 96; Central College, 88; Engineering Department, 92; Law Library, 92; Madison Hill, 91; No. 13, West Range "Rowdy Row", 46, 51; No. 33, West Range, 91; Old Rotunda clock, 96; Rotunda, *86*, 87-97

V

Venable, Col. Charles S., 96
Versailles, Kentucky, 15
Via, Vera, 64
Virginia Continentals, 11, 16
Virginia General Assembly, 14, 20
Virginia Military Institute, 73
Virginia Navy, 13
Virginia State Guard, 125
Virginia, Provisional Army, 80

W

Waddell, W. B., 75, 76
Wade, Jeptha, 80
Walker, Dr. Thomas, 17
Wall Street, 101
Warren County, Virginia, 103, 104
Warwick, Virginia, 46
Washington D. C., 25, 26, 28, 35, 36, 81, 88, 107, 121
Washington *Daily Intelligencer,* 35
Washington, Pres. George, 14, 30, 42, 121
Waynesboro, Virginia, 103
Webster, Daniel, 31
Wertenbaker, Charles C., 115, 123
Wertenbaker, William , 45, 49, 51
West Africa, 60, 63
West Point (U.S. Military Academy), 46, 75
White Hall, Virginia, 105
White House, 27
White, Rev. Rickey, 66
White, Samuel, 64
White, Stanford, 97

"William Wilson" by Edgar Allan Poe, 51, 52
Williamsburg, Virginia, 58
Willis, John, 46
Willis, Nellie, 29
Wilson, Dr. Gordon, 93
Winchester, Virginia, 117
Wolftown, Virginia, 106
Wood, Col. James, 16
Woodford County, Kentucky, 20
Woolen Mills, 63
World War II, 115, 122
Wright Jr., Marcellus, 107
Wright, Frances, 30

Y

Yellow fever epidemic, 33